The
Classic Guide
to
CYCLING

The Classic Guide to CYCLING

Rt-Hon Lord of Albemarle
&
G. L. Hillier

AMBERLEY

This edition published 2015

Amberley Publishing
The Hill, Stroud
Gloucestershire, GL5 4EP

www.amberley-books.com

Copyright © Amberley Publishing, 2015

British Library Cataloguing in Publication Data.
A catalogue record for this book is available from the British Library.

ISBN 978 1 4456 5091 3 (print)
ISBN 978 1 4456 5092 0 (ebook)

Typesetting and Origination by Amberley Publishing.
Printed in the UK.

Contents

	Introduction	7
1	Historical	71
2	Riding	137
3	Dress	165
4	Cycling for Ladies	187
5	The Hygiene of Cycling	199

Introduction

Cycling is by far the most recent of all the sports treated of in the Badminton Library, there is none which has developed more rapidly in the last few years, nor is there any which has assumed a more assured position in popular favour. Professor Huxley said in his farewell address to the Royal Society a short time ago, that since the time of Achilles no improvement had added anything to the speed or strength attainable by the unassisted powers of man. The statement is true in the sense which the Professor no doubt attached to his words, that neither the stature nor the speed of man had improved since Homer's day, but it is no less true that a man by his unassisted powers can propel one of the machines with which we are now familiar at a pace which would have put Achilles to shame, and over distances which would have utterly amazed the heroes of the Homeric world. The circumstances attending this revolution – for such indeed it is – cannot be considered unworthy of record, and the following pages are an attempt to perform the task.

England may be looked upon as the home of cycling, the national habit of organisation which our countrymen possess in an eminent degree, and the national love for every form of strong personal exertion, combine to make it a pursuit in every way adapted to the taste of our people. The shady lanes of the south country, and the hilly roads of the north, appear to offer equal attraction, and now, though scarcely ten years have elapsed since the first bicycle made its appearance, there are few districts in which some form of cycle is not a familiar object.

In the streets of our great cities and in highways and byways throughout the land, carriages, swift and serviceable, propelled by the power of human muscles alone, have become common. The sight of a traveller of either sex, seated on a light machine, and proceeding with considerable rapidity and apparently but little exertion, is so usual that the wayfarer hardly turns his head to look at the accustomed sight. Yet it is but a very short time ago that the passage of a cyclist was wont to produce an exhibition of considerable excitement, and sometimes even demonstrations of hostility.

It is however not only as a means of locomotion that the cycle has produced a change in this and many foreign countries. The manufacture of these carriages has caused a considerable trade to come into existence, and a new and very exciting mode of racing has been added to the sports of the world. The historian of cycling has therefore something to say of it as a trade, as a sport, and as a pastime. Beyond this, again, there is something to be said as to the social organisation to which it has given rise, and the not inconsiderable industry to which the requirements of the cycling public give employment outside the limits of the cycle-builder's factory. It is difficult to say, with any approach to accuracy, what number of persons come within the designation of cyclists. In the year 1885 I set on foot some inquiries which led to the conclusion that they then numbered around 400,000. The estimate is a rough one, but it must still not be considered quite in the light of a random guess. For it is founded on the reports of an organisation of which the reader who will accompany me through the following pages will hear a good deal, the Cyclists' Touring Club, a body which has chief officers in every large town, and minor officials in every considerable village in England, and is therefore quite able to make an approximate estimate sufficiently accurate for our purpose.

The volume now in the reader's hand is designed not only to interest the general reader, but to form a useful handbook for all who are interested in any of the various ramifications of cycling. The intending purchaser may consult it as to the points about which he should satisfy himself before concluding his bargain. The racing man will find his prowess recorded, and be able to fight his battles over again, the tourist will discover all that can help him to prepare for his intended outing, the advice given being founded on the accumulated experience of many predecessors. The young amateur who possesses a turn of speed, and proposes to become a candidate for the honours of the 'cinder-path,' will find minute directions as to his training and general preparations. The mechanic, and the rider who is interested in the details of the construction of his machine, will read descriptions of all the processes by which iron, steel and silver are made to assume the shape of the graceful piece of mechanism which adds so largely to the power of locomotion possessed by unaided muscles.

Though there are many fancy varieties which do not come under either category, cycles fall generally into two divisions: those with three wheels and those with two. Riders also arrange themselves into two sharply defined classes: the speedy bicycle rider and the more staid possessor of the tricycle. The racing man comes in as a connecting link between the two, for almost as many races are ridden on one class of machine as on the other. The enormous improvements introduced within the last year or two in the tricycle have made the tricycle as available, if not quite so speedy, as the bicycle for racing purposes. As regards speed, there is a considerable, though not an overwhelming, difference between the two. A really first-class bicycle rider – anyone who is sufficiently prominent in the pursuit to hold his own in a long-distance championship race – can travel, when at his best, considerably over 20 miles within the hour, only one tricycle rider has yet accomplished 20 miles in the hour. But it has been done several times by tandems. It is evident that machines which can maintain such a rate of progression must be sufficiently fast to make a race between well-matched competitors amusing: and those who have been fortunate enough to witness a well-contested race will be the first to testify that it lacks none of the elements of excitement and of sport.

One of the questions most frequently asked by those who intend to purchase a machine is, 'What pace can a reasonable person expect to get out of it?' and 'what distance can conveniently be covered in a day?' The answer, naturally, varies very much according to the strength and skill of the person interrogated, but it is a fair question and deserves a candid answer. The Records Committee of the National Cyclists' Union can show duly authenticated performances which the average rider can only look at with respectful astonishment, 300 miles have been ridden on an ordinary high road by a wonderful young athlete on a bicycle, within twenty-four consecutive hours, and 264 miles have been covered on a tricycle within the same time. 100 miles have been travelled by a bicyclist on a cinder racing path in 5 hours, 50 minutes and 51 seconds. 50 miles were ridden by Messrs A. J. Wilson and G. P. Mills, on a tandem, in 2 hours, 46 minutes and 3 seconds, along the Great North Road. The 'best on record' for a single mile, at the moment these lines are penned, is for a bicycle 2 minutes and 31 seconds, and for a tricycle 2 minutes and 41 seconds. Before this book is in the hands of the reader these times will very likely have been surpassed, for every day sees new and important, though minute, improvements in the construction of machines, and though riders may not be better than their predecessors, they are good enough to take advantage of all improvements that are offered to them. But the foregoing of course are extraordinary performances. The question is what an ordinary mortal can do.

One of the writers jointly responsible for the present work – need it be concealed that it was the author of this introductory chapter? – Recently asked his colleague, in a careless manner, the following question: 'How far ought an ordinary man, in fair condition, to be able to ride easily in a day?' And the other made answer and said, with the air of a man who was absolutely giving himself away, 'If he intends to keep it up, say, for a week, he ought only to do a moderate day's work on the first day, say a 100, or a 120 miles, of course he can increase his distance as he gets into condition.' The present writer agreed with the speaker. 'Yes,' he said, 'a man ought to restrain his ardour at first, he ought not to attempt to do more than a 120 miles on the first day.' He refrained from confessing – though perhaps it was disingenuous to do so – that he himself looked back with some exultation to his own 'best on record', which amounts to 36 miles in one day, and he takes this opportunity of copying from his private journal a few lines which have unconsciously assumed the form of an affidavit or vow. They run as follows:

And the said deponent further maketh oath and saith, that if he, the said deponent, *suadente diabolo*, shall at any time hereafter attempt to cut, break, surpass, or otherwise defeat, the said record of 36 miles in one solar day, he hereby giveth to any witness of such attempt, be the said witness credible or otherwise, free leave to mention the fact. And the said deponent doth further declare, that he is credibly informed, and doth sincerely believe, that many persons who make a great fuss about cycling have never done so much.

But this is a digression: there is no use in saying that sort of thing to a man who has ridden 146 miles in 10 hours, and who holds half a dozen championships besides. A moderate rider, not being an athlete or a flier on the one hand, nor exceptionally weak on the other, can, when he is in practice, get over in an 1 hour and 7 minutes or 8 miles of ground on a tricycle and from 9 to 10 on a bicycle without much exertion, and can keep it up about as long as he could comfortably walk with the same amount of exertion, say 4 or 5 hours. But there are many who cannot do so much as that, and who still manage to get a good deal of amusement out of their pursuit. Persevering riders cover enormous distances in the course of a year, and as most of them keep some sort of riding journal, we hear from time to time what their performances have been. A letter now before us from Mr Whatton, a well-known member of the Cambridge University Club, contains the following paragraph:

The year has been memorable to me as an individual in one or two respects. The early part of it saw the completion of 20,000 miles of cycling, the work of eight years' pleasure – pleasures that no other bodily exercise, unless it be racquets, can approach and that lacks the great glory of cycling, the multitudinous opportunities it adds for an intellectual and, may one add, a spiritual appreciation of life.

This is the proper spirit in which to look at the pastime of cycling as it may be followed by ordinary individuals, though it is not everyone who can ride 20,000 miles. It is, however, not only for amusement that cycling is available, both in the pursuit of health and of business it is of great value. In many parts of the country labourers are able to live at a considerable distance from their work, and mechanics are to be seen in considerable numbers with their tool-bags slung at their backs riding home at the end of their day's labour. Not only does this imply a saving of rent – for it is cheaper to live in the country than in the crowded town – but it is a distinct gain both in health and, in many instances, in sobriety as well. The wife and children of a mechanic are sure to be healthier if they live in the pure air of the country than in the crowded streets of a town. Rates and taxes are less and, regarding sobriety, a man who has to make his way home over 10 or a dozen miles of road will be pretty sure not to handicap his chance of a safe arrival by lingering too long at the public house. In Coventry, which may be looked upon as the peculiar home of cycling, it is fast becoming the custom for workmen to go home on their bicycles during the dinner-hour.

As a vehicle for business purposes the tricycle has even a larger future before it than the bicycle. It will carry a considerable quantity of luggage, and can be drawn up to the side of the street and left unprotected until the owner returns.

The number of shopkeepers who employ the carrier tricycle for the purpose of distributing their parcels, or circulating daily supplies to their customers, is steadily increasing. The milkman, the newsvendor, the butcher, send an active lad on their daily rounds. For light parcels it is especially adapted, and there has even been talk of establishing, in London, a service of tricycle cabs – machines like bath chairs with a rider behind.

One is tempted to say with Horace:

Illi robur et aes triplex,
Circa pectus erat, qui fragilem truci,
Commisit –

But hold: '*pelago ratem*' will not convey my meaning and I fear '*Pall-Mallo Bath-chairum*' would neither scan nor construe. Harrogate, well known to cyclists as the scene of the Annual Cycling Camp, has already shown the way in this respect. There the terrors of the streets are disregarded, even the steep pitches of the hills appear to have no deterrent effect. There, among the long row of Bath chairs drawn up for hire, may always be found three or four Coventry chairs. They appear very popular, and may be seen on fine afternoons in all the walks and drives round the fashionable watering-place, with their freight of invalids. If smiling faces and rosy cheeks may be trusted as an indication, the use of them is not confined to those who have the excuse of ill-health for adopting them. It is, no doubt, much more amusing even to an invalid to travel at a decent speed of 6 or 7 miles an hour, and to get over a considerable stretch of road, than to crawl, at the pace of a walking funeral, backwards and forwards along the length of a parade. At Harrogate one sees parties of three or four of these machines going along in company, the occupants of the chairs are able to converse in comfort, and the drivers encourage each other up the hills, which, as cyclists acquainted with Harrogate know, are not to be despised. They go long distances too. A lady mentioned to the present writer that she had just returned from an expedition in one of the chairs to Fountains Abbey, 9 miles away and her driver told her that he often took his customers similar or even longer distances without thinking anything of it. I asked whether the man had dismounted at the hills, which are on that road long and steep, the lady had not observed whether he had done so. I could not help thinking, though I did not give audible changed places with the driver for half a mile, the hills would have occupied a somewhat different place in her memory.

In our opinion, after seeing the practical working of these chairs at Harrogate, the ordinary form of that vehicle must die out. A thoughtful mind may not unreasonably wonder what will become of the very old and decrepit persons who now man Bath chairs. The sole qualification for the post seems to be great feebleness and very restricted powers of locomotion, and it must be confessed that a Coventry-chair rider must be in possession of at least average physical strength. But, after all, great as are the advantages of tricycles for business purposes, their principal claim on the gratitude of mankind is the large amount that is added by their means to the sum of human happiness. No one can fail to observe that such is the case who will take the trouble to station himself at one of the chief arterial outlets of any great city, and watch the stream of people going away into the country for their Saturday to Monday holiday. He who will take his stand on the bridge at Kew, or at Highgate Archway, will see a perfect stream of cycles speeding away into the country. Not only is there a light brigade of young men, bent on some favourite country resort 40 miles away or more, but steady middle-aged citizens on sober tricycles, some of them on sociables, with wife or daughter at their side, are bound on less distant expeditions. As regards the younger men, it is more than probable that the light and swift machines upon which they are mounted make all the difference to them whether they pass the brief holiday at the week's end in the stifling city or among the free breezes and shady lanes of the country, and the advantage both to morals and health can hardly be over-estimated. Among young ladies, the tricycle is a source of enjoyment. It is better for any young creature with sound limbs and healthy spirits to speed away over heaths and downs than to pore over a novel under the trees, or even to play lawn tennis on one eternal acre of grass-plot. It may be said that there are few country houses where some form of cycle is not to be found. The young ladies have their light machines, the boys have their bicycles, and in the stables there is sure to be found a bicycle belonging to some active young footman who will be delighted to get the chance to carry a note and bring back the answer in shorter time than it would take the groom to saddle a horse. No one who thinks of the confined indoor life led habitually by domestic servants would grudge him the outing.

If royal and imperial example count for anything, the practice will soon be universal, for there is not a crowned head in Europe who has not a stud of these useful iron steeds. Whether the grandees of Middle Europe personally career about the well-trimmed allies of their royal castles I do not know, but we may at least, from custom and precedent, infer the existence in dignified leisure of many a Kaiserliche-Konigliche Hochoberhoffvelocipedenkurator.

The Khedive of Egypt has several tricycles, one in particular, which I have had the honour of inspecting, is so covered with silver plating, that one can hardly see the black enamel it is supposed to adorn. It will doubtless come in handy should His Highness take it into his head to ride across the Bayuda Desert. He would there 'scorch' after a fashion not contemplated by the North Road Club. The officials of that body should look to this seriously and without delay. No one knows more accurately than Mr A. J. Wilson the perversity, to call it by no harsher name, of the NCU executive, and if any claim were founded on His Highness's performance, backed as it might easily be by French or Russian intrigue, and such claim were disallowed by the Records Committee, no one can foretell the political complications that might arise. 'Faed' should at once communicate with the official time-keeper, and arrange that at least His Highness's watch shall be properly compared at the Kew Observatory, under NCU rules. Among gorgeous tricycles some of the Indian princes possess vehicles which will hold their own, though after seeing the Khedivial state tricycle, I cannot affirm that they are pre-eminent. I have seen a picture in which the Maharajah, or an Indian state, together with the British resident at his court (an enthusiastic cyclist whose predilections perhaps somewhat influenced the royal taste), and all the great officers of the durbar are seated on tricycles at the gate of the palace, and gaze at the lens of the camera with the breathless attention usual on such occasions. They present an odd effect of costume. Wearers of shawls and jewelled turbans sit on some of the tricycles, British shooting jackets and knickerbockers figure on others. I understood from the possessor of the picture that the whole party were going out for a 'club run', and that His Highness is the president of that institution.

One of the great advantages of the tricycle over its two-wheeled rival is that it permits the rider to stop at will. A bicycle, on the contrary, only retains its stable equilibrium on the condition of being kept in constant motion. An attempt at a halt is instantly rewarded by an upset. An active rider can dismount very quickly, but an elderly gentleman, however skillful he might be, would feel the impossibility of performing the necessary gymnastics if he should be so ill-advised as to ride a bicycle through crowded streets. The construction of the bicycle also makes it an impossible mount for ladies, to whom the tricycle offers no sort of difficulty. For town work and for the use of the gentler sex the tricycle is decidedly the more convenient machine. On country roads, and for young and active riders, it is a matter of taste which should have the preference.

Although the advantages and pleasures of cycling are open to all able-bodied persons, the choice of a machine is a matter of individual preference. Practically no one would ever hesitate to decide under which category, bicyclist or tricyclist, he himself ought properly to come. A lady, a middle-aged man, or a heavy father, will naturally go in for a tricycle. An active lad, especially if he lives in the country, would probably give his voice for the bicycle, unless, indeed, he had reached the age or attained to the condition of mind which might prompt him to invest in a 'sociable', on the chance of inducing some adorable being of the gentler sex to share his pilgrimage on wheels.

There is another form of double tricycle which has lately come into fashion, principally among racing men, in which two performers sit one behind the other on the backbone of the machine, and pedal in unison. This is known as a tandem. The pace to be got out of this sort of vehicle is very great, and it will no doubt be still further improved, but it can hardly be said that to an outsider it looks very comfortable. There is also a horrible engine in existence known as a bicycle-tandem. It is formed by joining the large wheels of two full-sized bicycles one behind the other with a stout bar of iron between them, on which two saddles are fitted. It is said to be capable of being driven at a speed exceeding anything else on wheels. '*Il faut respecter tous les goûts*', as the French proverb teaches us, but providence will surely so far intervene as to prevent the general public from succumbing to its attractions. I am bound to add that, with the 'owner (and inventor) up' in company with some efficient coadjutor, this machine is capable of being so handled as almost to convince the spectator that to ride it is neither dangerous nor difficult, but then Mr Rucker is not only a very clever and a very persuasive gentleman, but a first-rate rider as well. Full descriptions of every kind of cycle will be found in the following pages, and it is not now necessary to dwell upon them at length. Almost all the machines that now compete for public favour partake of the wonderful qualities of lightness combined with strength which is the distinguishing characteristic of modern workmanship.

It is remarkable how quickly both the bicycle and the tricycle after their first inception assumed the form which they have since retained. It is hardly too much to say that no material change has been made in the type of either kind of machine, though the new 'dwarf' and 'safety' bicycles may not improbably be found to herald a new departure. But it is yet too soon to speak positively on this point. As regards the ordinary bicycle and tricycle, improvements in detail have been numerous and important, subsequent makers still adhere very closely to the broad lines laid down by the first designers. This is the more remarkable, because it can hardly be supposed that the original form was reasoned out on strict mathematical principles. It would almost seem that the proportions of the original design were hit upon by intuitive perception rather than by close adherence to rule. But it is a curious fact that the more the question is subjected to scientific investigation, the more patent does it become that the first attempts embodied correct mechanical ideas. Of course I speak only of the type of machine now so common, and not of the various 'velocipedes' as they were called, which enjoyed a short-lived popularity before the present class of cycles came into existence. In our account of what may be called the history of cycling, we shall show what the precursors of modern cycles were like. The Draisnene, the hobby horse, the dandy horse, and the four-wheeled velocipedes, resembled the modern cycle principally in that they all utilise the power of human muscles as a motive agent, in the principles of their construction they differed entirely from the cycle of today. But when the first bicycle was made it came complete and perfect from the maker's hand. The new type differed from any mechanical adaptation that had ever been thought of before and the idea, once embodied in a machine, has since been improved constructively only the principle, so far as anything mundane can be so, is perfect of its kind. The theory embodied in the machine is this: the bicycle consists of a large front wheel with pedals attached to its hub, over which the rider sits and works upright, his saddle is arranged on a bar of iron, which droops like a tail from the head to the ground, the end of it supported by a small trailing wheel, which bears a part of the rider's weight and prevents him from falling backwards. In the case of the tricycle all this is changed: the rider sits on a saddle, suspended above the axle, between two wheels of moderate size and a third point of contact with the ground is afforded by a smaller wheel, which, like the bicycle trailing wheel, bears a portion of the weight, the third wheel sometimes follows, but more often precedes the other two. The rider's seat is arranged either slightly in front of, or behind, the axle, according to the position of the third wheel, which serves the purpose of a rudder, and gives to the machine the name of front or rear steerer, as the case may be. In the case of the tricycle, as the rider rests on three points, he need not trouble himself about his balance, which is secure whether the carriage is in motion or not. This is the main point which makes the tricycle easier to ride than the bicycle, the rider need not dismount when it is necessary for any reason to come to a halt. He sits still and 'waits till the clouds roll by.' Nor is he compelled to maintain his balance by the sway of his body, he sits quiet and guides the machine by the movement of his wrists on the steering gear.

Falling forwards from a bicycle is by no means a difficult exploit – indeed, the difficulty is to avoid performing it. The manoeuvre is so common that the peculiar form of tumble that ensues is known by the distinctive name of 'the cropper,' or 'imperial crowner'. The habitual recurrence of the imperial crowner is prevented by placing the rider's saddle a trifle behind the centre of gravity of the machine: his balance is secured, when the machine is in motion, by guiding the driving wheel slightly in the direction to which his weight inclines, in exactly the same manner as a skater executes his long and graceful curves on the outside edge. After a certain amount of practice, the skillful bicyclist ceases to think of his steering handles any more than a skater does of his skates. In both cases the steering is regulated by subtle action of the muscles, but in the case of the cyclist, as in that of the skater, so far as conscious action is concerned, his course is determined by the poise and sway of his body.

Endless are the stories told by bicyclists of the curious and complicated falls which are thus executed 'over the handles'. Of them, as of Cleopatra's charms, we may say 'age cannot wither them nor custom stale their infinite variety.' A few, but fortunately very few, have terminated fatally. More frequently the active lads who form the main body of bicycle riders escape with bruises only, and learn caution from their escapes. The Hon. Arnold Keppel, late of the Scots Guards, had, when a lad, two most remarkable tumbles. Concerning which, in reply to an inquiry for particulars, he writes as follows:

In the year 1876 I was returning by night from Worthing with two friends to Storrington, in Sussex, where we were reading for the Army examinations. We were each riding a 54 inch Coventry Machinist bicycle. There was only one lamp among the party, and the owner of this was told off to ride in front. There is a long hill on this road, down which we had to come, and the night was very dark. Our friend with the lamp was 50 yards ahead, going at a great pace, when on nearing the bottom of the hill he saw a horse and fish-cart coming in the opposite direction. He had just time to go between the hedge and the cart. The horse was scared and turned suddenly right across the road. I was next and less fortunate than our leader, I struck the shaft of the cart fair and square. Before I had time to realise the situation I found myself lying in the road on the other side, the machine and I having fallen clear over the 'horse. The marvel was that not a bolt was sprung in the machine, and the only evidence it bore of a collision was a dent and scratches on the top nut of the head. I did not break my neck, but I broke my nose, and sustained other cuts and bruises which it is needless to particularise. I must confess that, if I have to tumble, I prefer to take my chance of the vicissitudes of the hunting-field.

The other tumble about which you ask sounds too like 'a yarn' for me to risk my reputation by narrating it. G. H. [naming a friend and relation, then a fellow-student at Storrington, and now an officer in the Life Guards] says positively that he saw it happen. I cannot be considered an eye-witness, for I remember nothing till I found myself in a cottage, being 'brought to' with restoratives.

The header in question came about in the following fashion: The Storrington Army students were holding a race meeting among themselves, and the competitors were taking a preliminary canter before the start. Mr Keppel, going best pace through a lane of spectators, ran over a piece of coal which had fallen from a passing cart. The machine turned a somersault, so complete a somersault that the rider came uppermost again, and the wheel went on several yards before it finally fell. Mr Keppel, though still in the saddle, was unconscious of anything, as he says in his letter, from the moment his head and shoulders touched the earth. The handles of the machine were bent upwards in a very extraordinary manner.

The 'Imperial crowner' is of comparatively frequent occurrence. Dogs, pigs, fowls, and children share the honour of causing it. A course of bricks or a string across a road placed in the course of an approaching cyclist by playful youth has not unfrequently produced it, and the British rough has discovered that a stick inserted into the moving wheel frequently inflicts sufficient damage to give the assailant time to escape bodily chastisement by flight.

There seems to be hardly any limit to the skill that can be acquired by assiduous practice on the bicycle, and the exhibitions of address and daring which sometimes take place often take one's breath away. The following appeared in the English 'Bicycling News' of October 10 1886. I reproduce it in a slightly curtailed form, and before doing so have had the curiosity to inquire whether the event referred to really happened. I was informed that it actually occurred as described, and that the machine ridden on the occasion was a Star bicycle, the peculiarity of which is that the small wheel is in advance and steers the machine, while the weight of the rider rests mainly on the large driving-wheel, which is of the same dimensions as an ordinary full-sized bicycle, around fifty or fifty-two inches. This make of bicycle has enthusiastic admirers in America, and it may be noted that the extraordinary trick-riders, Kauffman and McAnney, who exhibited in 1886 at the Westminster Aquarium, performed their wonders upon it:

A daring and foolhardy feat was performed by a bicyclist the other afternoon at Cabin John Bridge, near the city, says a Washington telegram to the *Pittsburg Dispatch*. The place is a general pleasure resort about 12 miles from town, over the military road built by Jefferson Davis while Secretary of War. The bridge is said to be the largest single span of masonry in the world.

It is 125 feet high, and about 200 feet long, a single magnificent arch spanning a deep and rocky gorge. A good many people go out there to see the bridge and the man who keeps the little hotel known as Cabin John, just at the end and across the bridge, does a good business – especially on Sunday. Every nice Sunday the sheds about the place are crowded with vehicles of every description, and sporting men, family parties, wheelmen, and gentlemen of leisure, are loafing about the house, getting country dinners or picnicking in the wild gorge below the bridge. As at all such places, there are always a few wheelmen lounging in and out, and a number of machines were stacked about the yard that afternoon, and a lively party within could be heard telling stories and boasting of their personal skill on the road. In the midst of the hilarity one young man suddenly came out alone, and, singling out his machine, mounted, and without a word rode towards the bridge. There is a brownstone coping on the three-foot wall on either side of the roadway. This coping is about a foot broad, and is bevelled on the two upper edges for an inch or two. On the inside of these walls is the solid roadway above the duct. On the outside is a perpendicular descent of about 125 feet in the centre of the bridge, and no less than 75 feet at either abutment. The young man stopped and dismounted at the end of the bridge and lifted his machine upon the coping. The act was noticed by a couple of gentlemen smoking under the trees, but it was looked upon as a freak, and no particular attention was paid to it. The next moment there was an exclamation of horror, for the young man was seen mounted upon his bicycle deliberately riding along the narrow coping. The sight froze the blood of the ladies and children picnicking in the gorge below, and was enough to appall the stoutest heart. The gentlemen in front of the hotel started to their feet and called to the other wheelmen within. It was too late. The young man was already in the centre of the bridge. He never swerved a hair's breadth from his seat. From the end of the bridge he seemed a toy machine running by mechanism, so erect and motionless he sat, and so evenly he rode. 'Let him alone,' cried one of his companions, 'he could ride it if it was a rope!' Nevertheless, the fear that interference might hasten the horror that all wished to prevent left the party rooted to the spot. In two places the coping makes a zigzag by the widening of the roadway, and at these places the rider must steer his wheel through a very narrow space at nearly right angles with his course. The daring fellow had passed the first of these ticklish spots, and when he carefully wore round the second not a single one of the horrified spectators could draw a breath for fear. From thence to the end was a short and straight run, and in another moment the young man had completed his dangerous ride, dismounted, and was waving his hand laughingly at the frightened men and women and children who had witnessed it. The young fellow calmly remounted his wheel and rode on towards the city as if he had done a very common thing not worth mentioning. He was induced to undertake the feat because someone had doubted whether he had the requisite ability and nerve to perform it.

Kauffman and his companion McAnney, mentioned above, executed wonders almost beyond belief. One of their feats, though I witnessed it several times, still appears to me when I think of it almost incredible. Kauffman brought into the arena a common but strongly-built kitchen table, upon it he placed two chairs, one to receive the front wheel of his bicycle and the other the hind wheel. He then mounted on the table, climbed on to the chairs, and from thence slowly and carefully, with almost imperceptible motions, balancing his unstable mount the while, crept up the spokes of his machine and finally stood upright on the saddle, at a height of 12 or 14 feet from the ground. The newspapers tell us from time to time that he is still performing to large and enthusiastic audiences in various parts of Europe, so that it may be supposed that he has not yet broken his neck. I asked the performer at the close of one of his performances whether in his learning stage he had fallen or hurt himself much, his reply was somewhat characteristic: 'No, sir,' he said, 'I perceived at a very early stage of my training that I should have to quit falling, so before I went any farther I trained myself to do that.'

'What do you mean?' said I, 'you cannot prevent an accident.'

'No,' said he with a smile, 'but I have trained myself so to keep my balance at every stage of the performance that a slip, even though it should take place at apparently the most critical point of the performance, would almost infallibly land me on my feet.' Several times he did fall – though not in the most dangerous feats, which were executed with extreme slowness of movement and care – and on each occasion he lighted, as he declared he would, on his feet.

It is needless to say that for people who are not in the enjoyment of that activity and elasticity which belongs mainly to youth, the tricycle presents many advantages. It has drawbacks, the machine is necessarily heavier in itself, as it has three wheels instead of two. It offers more resistance to obstacles on the road, and this is increased by the circumstance that in the case of the bicycle the two wheels follow each other, and so practically make only one track, whereas the three wheels of the tricycle make each a track of its own.

On the other hand, the tricycle can be made to carry a considerable amount of luggage, enough may be packed about the body of the carriage to supply the wants of a moderate-minded person for a tour of two or three days or even more. It is quite easy to stow away a bag weighing ten or twelve pounds. After all, a complete suit of flannels is all that a tourist absolutely requires, and the weight of such a kit is hardly felt on a tricycle. Many enthusiastic artists carry about a whole photographic outfit and it is darkly rumoured that the members of the Tricycle Union, a select body who are the objects of a good deal of harmless 'chaff' among the main body of cyclists and who love to combine various branches of science with their favourite pastime, secrete about the frame of their iron steeds all the paraphernalia of their several mysteries.

The late Sir Charles Napier used to declare that he considered a soldier amply provided if he started on a campaign with a piece of soap and a toothbrush. A bicyclist on a tour, unless he agrees with the hero of Scinde in his estimate of what are necessaries in life, can only provide for his requirements by elaborate prevision in the way of forwarding luggage to points ahead on the line of march. Bags christened by their inventors with the suggestive names of Saturday-to-Monday, or *multum-in-parvo*, can be obtained in great variety from the stores of cycling outfitters. These little valises are said (by the makers) to be amply sufficient for the wants of a travelling cyclist, but a kit, when packed in a *multum-in-parvo* bag, and strapped on the backbone of a bicycle, presents a very attenuated appearance, and a man's desires must be very strictly subordinated to the force of circumstances if he looks on such an outfit as sufficient.

One of the most remarkable characteristics of modern machines is the extreme lightness, it might almost be said the attenuation, of the parts of which they are composed. Every portion of the frame is made as strong and as light as possible, and the greatest mechanical ingenuity is shown in adjusting the shape of the various parts so as to produce the maximum of stability with the least possible weight. It is an established axiom in mechanical construction that, weight for weight, a hollow bar of proper form is stronger than solid metal. Advantage has been taken of this circumstance by cycle constructors, every part that can be made hollow is made so, and the resources of applied mechanics are exhausted to discover the form which most efficiently utilises the allotted material. For instance, the rims or felloes which are the steel peripheries of the wheels, and which serve to form the stiff and perfect outside of the circle, are hollow and though the exact form varies according to the taste of different manufacturers. They are all made by passing a tube of round steel between rollers of such construction that the tube is brought into a section of crescent form, the outer semilune serving for a bed to contain the thick rubber tires, which are also invariably employed.

It is worth the while even of even the most careless rider of cycles to pause for a moment over the construction of the suspension wheel. It is not too much to say that the ingenious invention, designated by that name alone, made it possible to construct the modern cycle. Before the invention of the suspension system wheels were made of light and strong hickory, or other wood, like the wheels of the ordinary carriages intended to be drawn by horses, which are still in use on the roads. On wooden wheels, the weight of the whole carriage rests on the particular spoke which happens to point perpendicularly downwards, and the stability of the wheel depends on the rigidity of that particular spoke. Exactly the reverse of this occurs in the case of the suspension wheel, in it the weight of rider and carriage rests on the centre of the wheel and is suspended from that part of the felloe which happens to be uppermost, by means of the spoke then most perpendicular.

The weight is thus constantly shifted from spoke to spoke as the wheel revolves, and the lateral spokes, being all braced tight, prevent the wheel from buckling, or getting out of shape. The result of this most ingenious arrangement is, that comparatively fine steel wire is substituted for a stiff wooden spoke, and the cycle wheel presents the beautiful and graceful, though apparently fragile, appearance which everyone no doubt has admired. In order to realise the magnitude of the revolution which this invention has brought about, it is only necessary to fancy what the appearance of a bicycle would be if it had wheels like even those of the lightest Victoria. Some enthusiasts have seen and ridden upon machines made after that fashion, but if it had not been reformed, cycling would never have attained its present popularity. Mr S. Maddison is said to have described, and Mr Edward Cooper to have been the first practically to use, the suspension wheel.

From the moment that the cycling Columbus broke the egg – from the moment, that is, that the inventors of the suspension wheel showed how a practical carriage could be made light enough to be worked easily by human muscles – manufacturers began to vie with each other in diminishing the weight of each minute part. This has been done with such assiduity, that at length, in the opinion of competent observers, the limits of attenuation have been pushed almost up to the borderline which divides safety from instability. It is now no longer necessary, as it was even a couple of years ago, to enjoin upon the maker of a machine to make it as light as possible. He is sure to do that. The necessity is rather that the rider should make sure that his mount is up to his weight. A hundred, or even 120 pounds, was recently not thought an unreasonable weight for a tricycle: but nowadays even these small weights are reduced by 20 or 30 pounds. The reader will of course understand that, whether the higher or the lower scale of weights is taken, the same type of machine will be made, by a good builder, considerably stronger and consequently heavier for a large man than for a small one. Indeed, to enjoy anything like the full amount of enjoyment that can be got out of the pastime of cycle riding, a man's machine should be built to his measure with the same solicitude that his tailor displays in producing his coat. It sounds like attributing selfishness to a very estimable class of persons to mention with approbation the fact that a practiced cyclist is very unwilling to lend his machine to anybody else, but such is the case. Alhough the non-cyclist may perhaps have tried a friend's machine without observing the look of agony with which the loan was unquestionably conceded, he may rest assured that, like the celebrated parrot, his friend, if he said little, thought a good deal.

A beginner who takes up cycling and does not, at first, find it as pleasant as he expected, should not give it up in despair until he has satisfied himself that he has fulfilled all the requirements which make success possible. He exercises a new set of muscles, so that after his first essays, even though he be a practiced athlete, he will certainly be stiff and uncomfortable. He will be certain to ride badly, he will turn out his toes, probably graze his ankles against the pedals, wriggle on his seat, twist his knees, or perform other cycling enormities, but even if he did not, there are obstacles which must be removed before success is possible. Even the winner of last year's championship could not ride 20 miles on a saddle that did not fit him, and that Great Being himself would stop from sheer agony, exhausted and leg weary, if his seat were at an inconvenient distance from his pedals, or, as he would probably himself phrase it, if he were not placed properly over his work. Let not the novice, therefore, whether of the gentle or of the sterner sex, be too easily discouraged. Let him ascertain, as may be done from a book as well as in any other way, what the essentials of the situation really are, and see that they are complied with, before giving way to the idea, erroneous in the great majority of cases, that in his case cycling is a forbidden luxury.

Actual demonstration and personal assistance of friends are useful. But almost as much is to be learned from books as from oral instruction. A book, unlike a friend, is always at hand with a complete account of the matter in all its bearings. Minute particulars assume a very different relative importance when the subject begins to be familiar than they did at first, and a matter at first dismissed or disregarded as unimportant can be referred to at leisure and reconsidered. Besides, in a book the accumulated and carefully noted experience of many beginners has been noted. A beginner, knowing nothing of details, does not know what information to ask for should a difficulty arise, the printed friend can always be summoned, which may possibly not be the case with the oral adviser.

But we are digressing from the subject of cycle building. The first point, as we said above, to ensure success and save a surgeon's bill, is to order a machine fully up to your weight, otherwise there will certainly be a breakdown, and probably an accident. Next take care that your machine fits you. If these points have been attended to, and the small amount of practice be taken which is necessary to accustom the muscles to the new labours they are called upon to undergo, there will be no inclination to drop the practice in disgust.

Though we are not now going to enter into a disquisition on the mechanical theory of progression as exemplified in cycle riding, it would be well that every rider and purchaser of a machine should keep the first principles of that theory in his mind.

Those who wish to pursue it in detail cannot do better than consult the work of Mr Warner Jones, a writer who very ably unites practical cycling and theory, to his scientific little treatise we refer readers interested in the mathematical bearings of the subject.

It will be sufficient for our present purpose to note that the science of progression as regards cycling, as in all applications of mechanics, consists in a due apportionment of quantities in an equation, which deals with the three factors, weight, force, and time. A machine with a rider upon it offers a certain weight or resistance to be moved. If the strength that the rider can put forth be measured, and his weight and that of his machine be ascertained, it only remains to calculate to what distance the force at disposal can move the weight in a given time.

If, when a carriage is in motion, it is desired to quicken the pace, the force employed must be increased, because from the conditions of the problem the weight is a fixed quantity and the time within which it is to be moved is diminished. But in the case of a rider who is already putting forth all his strength, the force cannot be increased, therefore as he cannot increase the driving power the rider must have a lighter machine, or be content to go more slowly. Every alteration of one factor is obtained only at the expense of another, increased resistance from hills for instance requires more power or less speed, probably both, and when the rider has 'put in all he knows', he comes to a standstill.

Hills are not the only obstacles that have to be overcome in cycling, and when the mud, ruts, stones, and the general surface of the road have to be taken into account, all these may be classed under the general name of resistance to the performance of the work required. The best solution of the equation is to reduce the weight of the cycle to the lowest point consistent with safety, to build the machine so as most effectually to minimise the friction of the road, and to utilise in the best possible manner the strength exercised by the rider.

The first point in designing a machine is to make it of such form that it shall offer the minimum of friction, and support the weight of the rider in an attitude which will enable him with the least effort to put forth all his strength.

A man's natural means of progression are designed by nature in such a manner as to afford him a power of advancing under all the circumstances under which he is likely to be placed. This is a roundabout way of saying that the human leg is, so to speak, a compromise that fulfils varying and sometimes opposite requirements. They are not constructed especially for speed, a pair of them will carry their possessor along a level road, across rough ground such as a swamp or a Scotch moor, or up an Alpine mountain. The bicycle or tricycle is designed to help him along under one condition only, that is, over a moderately even road. An athletic man, putting forth all his strength, could perhaps walk 5 miles along a level road or 3 miles across a stretch of grouse ground, within the hour. Mounted on a bicycle he could go 5 or even 20 miles in the same space of time, but if mounted on his bicycle and he transferred the scene of his operations to the moor or the mountain side, he would not advance a mile in a week. Yet the amount of force expended, supposing that he puts forth his utmost strength, must in each instance be the same, and the motion of his legs, whether in walking or in cycling, is substantially the same. The human limbs practically act like the spokes of a wheel, the thigh joint representing the hub, the leg on which the walker stands is the spoke perpendicularly beneath the centre, when he advances, the hindmost leg comes forward, and as the centre of gravity is shifted the human wheel rolls forward through a certain portion of its periphery. The same action takes place when the man travels on a tricycle, only in that case with the same amount of exertion he goes faster, because he has employed mechanical devices to overcome friction. Instead of taking a succession of springs and shifting his balance at every forward step, he has interposed between himself and the ground a continuous bearing surface, namely the tire of his cycle wheels, he has substituted a steady mechanical pressure for a forward jump, and his weight, steadily supported over the centre of gravity of the carriage, leaves his legs free to exert their strength to the greatest advantage, and adds momentum to his course in the exact direction of motion of the machine.

It hardly needs proof that if mechanical means are to be adopted to reduce friction, a wheel of some sort is the best device. It therefore only remains to consider what the size of the wheel is to be. The exact dimensions depend on the size of the obstructions that have to be overcome. A large wheel overcomes an obstacle more easily than a small one, as may be easily seen by moving the wheel of a child's toy cart against a brick, and then moving a carriage-wheel against the same object. The small wheel will stop dead short and the larger wheel will mount over it because in the first instance the whole, or the greater part of the circle, is behind the point of impact, and in the other a sufficient part of the circle is in front of the point of impact. This is not a scientific statement, because it does not take into consideration all the conditions stated, but it is sufficiently accurate for our purpose.

In practice, obstacles likely to be encountered on the road will probably not exceed 2, or at the most 3, inches in height. It is to be hoped that few stones of that size are ever found on a road if any are so placed, the road surveyor of the district ought to be summarily hanged. If ruts, mud, or anything else is encountered which exceeds 3 inches, the best plan for the cyclist who is condemned to meet such obstacles is to get off and walk till he reaches a part of the road that is under the management of a surveyor with some Christian feeling. But while the wheel must be made sufficiently large to surmount ordinary stones with ease, it must not be larger than is absolutely necessary. For not only is a large wheel unduly heavy but it offers more surface to the wind – and wind is almost harder for a cyclist to encounter than a rough or hilly road. The limit of size as regards to bicycles is affected by another consideration – the length of the rider's leg, and the limit of size in bicycle wheels is practically governed by that consideration. The same condition is also present in the case of tricycles, though in this case other circumstances must also be taken into account. The tricycle rider should, when sitting on the saddle with his leg extended, have the pedal on which his foot rests 3 or more inches from the ground, in order to clear the inequalities of the road. Mathematical considerations show that the centre of a wheel, which will support the weight of the rider in such a position as to enable him to put forth his utmost strength, should be about 24 inches from the ground. The saddle on which the rider sits is raised a few inches above the axle of the wheels, and as a matter of practice a 48-inch wheel has been found a convenient size. Recent experiments seem to indicate that a wheel of 40 inches in diameter is even better than 48. The decision will no doubt be made in the case of each rider on considerations which vary with individual tastes and requirements. There are some among the exponents of cycling who are hotly in favour of wheels greatly larger or smaller than this standard, just as there were, in the country discovered by Captain Gulliver, Bigendian convicts who were undergoing punishment for obstinately cracking the large ends of their eggs. But of their opinions we need take no note. Mathematical reasoning has also determined the theoretical best position for the smaller wheel of the tricycle, as may be seen at large in Mr Warner Jones's volume.

Up to a very recent period it was not possible to adopt the mechanical device called 'gearing up' to the bicycle, consequently it was necessary to have the driving wheel as large as possible consistently with the pedal being within easy reach of the rider's foot, in order that a single revolution of the wheel might cover as large a space of ground as possible. Any diminution of size of wheel necessitated faster pedalling or slower speed. Now that a means has been found to gear-up bicycle wheels to any required pitch, the large wheel is no longer found essential, and a change has apparently set in in favour of small wheels. Numerous forms of dwarf bicycle have lately appeared, and the marvellous performances that have been made by their aid on the road shows the value of the change.

We shall describe farther on the construction of 'dwarf' or 'safety' bicycles, as they are sometimes indiscriminately called. But the two terms are by no means convertible. Many of the dwarf bicycles now offered for sale, though they have merits of their own, are anything but 'safeties'. It is true that if you tumble you do not fall so far as from a high bicycle. Still one class alone, known as the 'Rover' type, offers immunity from the dreaded 'header'. And a machine of that type is now offered by a great many of the leading manufacturers. It is very desirable that the two terms 'dwarf' and 'safety' should not be confounded.

The term 'gearing up' occurred a few lines back, as it is a phrase which will be used often it may be as well to explain the meaning of the term. It is a well-known principle of mechanics that by the use of large and small toothed wheels acting upon each other, power may be obtained at the expense of speed or speed at the expense of power. This principle has been adapted recently both to bicycles and tricycles. The revolutions of the driving wheels can be increased as compared with the pedals, or diminished, at the will of the rider, who by the turn of a handle or the movement of a lever can throw either speed or power gear into action. Many machines are now furnished with apparatus by which the rider may drive his wheels 'level', that is one revolution of the wheel for one of the pedal, 'up', by which one revolution of the pedal produces more than one revolution of the driving wheel, resulting of course in increased speed, or 'down' by which a revolution of the pedal produces only a part of a revolution of the driving wheel, and power for hill climbing and the like is obtained, at the expense of speed. This is a practical exemplification of the truth stated above that when one factor of the equation, the strength of the rider, is a fixed quantity, either speed or power must be sacrificed when the other conditions of the problem are varied. But this part of the subject will be more fully treated in future chapters, it is only necessary here to say that the proportions and general form of the tricycle rest, not on caprice nor on mere guesswork, but on defined and well-understood rules.

When cycles began to increase and multiply in the land, it was natural that the riders of them should organise themselves and assume a corporate existence for mutual support and defence. This was no doubt a matter of more urgent necessity in the early days of cycling than it is now. Cyclists were, at first, looked upon with distrust if not with positive dislike. It is possible that bicyclists, who were the earliest exponents of the art, were more aggressive and made their presence felt more acutely than is now the case. It was some time before horses got accustomed to them, and at first it was the fashion among some of the younger men to cover their coats with braid and blow bugles in the streets. The dislike with which they were regarded, if not deserved by the great majority, was in some instances sufficiently well merited. But these customs have long been things of the past Cyclists now behave with the decorum of judges on the bench, the equine race seems to have made up its mind that there is nothing in it, and even in the wildest districts of the country the half-brick of welcome is now seldom heaved at the cycling stranger.

Though the number of wandering cyclists increases year by year, it is probable that none of them will ever again undergo the experience of an early martyr in the cause, who roused the wrath of the driver and guard of the St Albans coach, the latter worthy provided himself with a lasso, and when the cyclist tried as aforetime to race the coach, he found himself dexterously lassoed and dragged in the mud. That guard is reported to have discovered by practical experience that a cyclist is not outside the protection of the law, and the incident is generally supposed to have contributed considerably to the development of the institution, then, and for a short time afterwards, known as the Bicycle Union, now merged in the larger and more important body called the National Cyclists' Union.

The organisation, which was at first necessary for defence, was continued for convenience, and side by side with it there grew up another institution called the Cyclists' Touring Club.

They are independent of each other, but work together very harmoniously. The NCU undertakes the legislation and legal defence as well as what may be called the police of cycling, while the CTC, as its name implies, attends to everything that conduces to the comfort of cycling tourists.

The cycling public constantly finds itself in contact with all by-laws and regulations which affect locomotion. The NCU have been able to establish the fact that it is for the public convenience that they should be consulted whenever Parliamentary or local legislation deals with the question of street traffic. The relations between cyclists and the railway companies present another subject of attention, and the organisation of racing, race meetings, and championships, together with the legal business just mentioned, affords constant employment to the executive of the union.

The work of the union is divided into two main sections: the representation of cycling in its relation to Parliament, to other sports, or to the general public, and, the internal regulation of cycling itself. The first embraces all legal matters concerning the cycle and its use on public roads and highways, including questions relating to rights-of-way, legal obstruction, gate tolls, assaults, and other things affecting wheel riding throughout the country. The second embraces the promulgation of rules and regulations for racing, the establishment and management of the amateur bicycle and tricycle championships, and the general supervision of the innumerable complaints and appeals which incessantly arise.

A very successful system of local self-government has been adopted, by the formation throughout the country of local centres, by means of which the union maintains its central control without losing the practical usefulness which can only be acquired by detailed local knowledge of men and things. Several of these centres have been formed in the great centres of population throughout the country, and have worked well in practice. The union is governed by a council, composed of members of affiliated clubs, together with the honorary secretaries and chairmen of the local centres. Despire the operation of the union being intended for the benefit of cycling as a whole, no direct personal benefit is obtained by membership: it differs in this respect considerably from the other great cycling organisation, the CTC, in which membership certainly does secure considerable advantages.

We have mentioned that the unit of formation from which the National Union has been formed is the Cycling Club. Almost every town and large village has one of these institutions, which are formed according to the exigencies of local society, and flourish in proportion to the energy of the elected captain and honorary secretary. Each club, provided its rules are in accord with the model rules formulated by the National Society, has the right to send, in proportion to its numbers, one or more members to the council of the union.

The council meets at stated intervals and forms a very real and workable Parliament for the discussion of cycling affairs. The national love for discussion, and the considerable aptitude for speechifying shown by many of the members, find full opportunity of exercise at the monthly meetings, and the temptation to a somewhat florid and lengthy style of oratory is found by many ardent spirits too great to be resisted.

Time, fortunately, will not permit questions of mere detail to be discussed, and only matters in which some principle is involved are put on the agenda paper, details are left to the consideration of an executive elected from among the members, which meets weekly at headquarters. Before this body are brought in the first instance all complaints, appeals, and projects of cycling legislation. The system, order, and expedition with which a large amount of detail is examined and disposed of offers an example which might without any disadvantage be followed by more pretentious assemblies. The National Union rests on the widest basis of publicity, and commands general allegiance and support. There was a time, it is true, when it was threatened with dissensions from within. This danger was, perhaps, almost inseparable from the constitution of the society. The original organisation belonged to bicyclists, who were first in the field, and who, in fact, began to organise themselves before tricycling was invented. But the development of tricycling brought another and, as a rule, an older set of men to the front, who were not quite ready to acquiesce in the leadership which priority of possession had placed in the hands of their juniors in years. *Beati possidentes* was not unnaturally the motto of the bicyclists, and the situation was one which at first presented some obstacles to harmonious working. It seemed possible, at one time, that tricyclists would break off and form an organisation of their own. But wiser counsels prevailed, and the united association has now for some years past offered a solid front to the world. A large, and perhaps in the eyes of some persons an undue, amount of the attention of the executive is taken up with racing, but this is not to be regretted. Even those who do not care for racing in itself may agree that the racing path is the place where a new invention is sure to be tested to the utmost, and if the invention be really an advantage it will be adopted. The opinions of the best riders and the keenest wits are concentrated upon it, and if it successfully undergoes the severe tests to which it is sure to be subjected by racing experts, it will certainly be adopted by manufacturers, to the manifest advantage of the general body of riders who, if not so assisted, would have had to wait long ere the natural conservatism of the workshop was overcome, for new patterns mean fresh outlay of capital, and the re-modelling of existing traditions.

While the National Union takes under its cognisance the police, the legal defence, and the legislation of cycling, there devolves upon a kindred, but at the same time quite a separate, institution, the care of individual comfort. The CTC exists for the mutual aid and protection of those among its members who travel along the Queen's highway, and sojourn temporarily in the towns and villages along its course. Although the rules of the club contain the usual provisions for the election of president, vice-presidents, and other officers of a large organisation, all these dignified posts are vacant, and the club flourishes under the control of an energetic and most efficient secretary, assisted, rather than controlled, by a somewhat shadowy council. It is true that at long intervals, once or twice a year, the secretary is called upon to meet the council of the club. He often passes through several – perhaps eight or nine consecutive – *mauvais quarts d'heure de Rabelais*, during which he listens to the bottled-up grievances of 20,000 members, detailed by their choicest grumblers. But, like the lead-keeled racing yachts that one sees in the Thames, he lies down on his beam-ends and lets the storm blow over him. When the council adjourns, the secretary resumes his sway, and continues to rule despotically – till next meeting.

The Touring Club, like the National Union, was founded by bicyclists. It was formed in the provinces in the year 1878, and was enlarged to include tricyclists in 1882. The defined objectives of the club are to promote touring by bicycles and cycles among amateurs (a term which has supplied an endless source of dispute both to the NCU and the CTC), and arrange for mutual defence, assistance and support. The plan of operation is as follows: a map of the British Isles is divided into districts, twelve of which are in England, four in Ireland, and seven in Scotland, and each is placed under the charge of an officer called a chief consul. This consular system is quite original. The chief consul, chosen always for his special knowledge of the requirements of cycling, selects assistants, known as consuls, from among the local members of the club, in the towns and villages of the district. He also appoints hotel headquarters, conducts correspondence with members asking information, attends the meetings of the council, and generally is responsible for the interests and working of the club in his immediate district. Consuls acting under the direction of their chief give information as to the state of the roads, and the places of interest within the district, to any member applying for it. They are expected to assist the chief consuls in filling up any vacancies that may occur in the list of hotels or repairing smiths, to look up subscriptions in arrear, and to secure new adherents for the club. All this organisation having been achieved, the chief consuls, consuls, hotel headquarters, recommended houses and repairing smiths appointed, the result is embodied in a handbook which, after being carefully revised every year, is supplied to members at a nominal charge. In any strange place, if a member's machine breaks down, he is assaulted, or in any way wronged, even if he is only benighted, he sees by a glance at his handbook who is the nearest friend to whom he can apply, where he can sleep and eat, and where he can get his damages repaired. The cases are few within the British Isles where a member of the CTC cannot get all his wants supplied by his own club, within a 4 or 5 mile distance from the place where any misadventure occurs to him. A member wishing to travel in any direction through the country, applies to the chief consul of the district through which his intended journey lies, and obtains every information necessary respecting roads, hotels, best route to pursue etc., besides being speeded on his way by the consuls of the chief towns through which he passes: for part of a consul's duty is to keep a watchful eye to the comfort and interest of any touring members who may be temporarily sojourning in the hotel headquarters. These last are by no means the least important part of the organisation, the club has either headquarters or recommended houses in all the chief towns and large villages of the kingdom. Recommended houses, as opposed to hotel headquarters, are houses which can in many cases hardly be designated hotels. Sometimes they are snug roadside inns in remote country villages. In such places it is often of great importance to the wet or belated traveller to find rest, refreshment, and recognition, even though a sanded parlour may be the only sitting-room, and a smiling maid may represent boots and waiter. The proprietor of a CTC house enters into a contract with the club, specifying that he will at all times 'receive and entertain any members of the club, whether ladies or gentlemen, who produce a valid ticket of membership for the then current year, and that he will charge them a tariff of prices,' which the contract then proceeds to set forth.

These agreements are mutually beneficial. They suit the innkeeper, because to him it means practically the monopoly of the trade to be done with cyclists, the number of whom would hardly be believed. Many hotels fell into sleepiness and decay when railroads took the place of coaches, and have now through the medium of cycling tourists revived, and do a profitable business, though teams of galloping posters have disappeared for ever. But the arrangement is by no means one-sided. The cyclist also profits by it. He is a new creation, his wants are novel and strange, and a specimen of the class descending on an hotel not specially prepared for his reception would probably cause more consternation than delight. The cyclist's hours are uncertain, he is as likely as not to arrive in the middle of the night, or long before breakfast. Whatever the hour of his arrival, he is quite certain to be very tired, very hungry, and very hot. He will have very little luggage, and though he should arrive at midday, he will certainly want to go to bed, not necessarily to sleep, but for the practical reason that bed is the best place for him to wait in while his clothes are being dried. To the good people at a cycling inn, these vagaries are the merest matters of routine, equally a matter of course is the request of the guest to be called and have breakfast ready at an unearthly hour of the morning, for the favourite plan of the younger spirits, who go careering over the country at the rate of 80 or a 100 miles a day, is to get over thirty or forty of them before breakfast. Great is the convenience to these young athletes of finding houses all over the country at which their requirements are studied, and their arrival hailed not only with cheerfulness but with welcome, and many are the travellers who have found the little silver badge of the club a passport to cheery kindness, which no agreement for special tariffs would alone suffice to secure.

Nor is it only the young athletes of rapid journeys and abnormally early hours who may benefit by the CTC agreement. It is not necessary for a member to avail himself of all his privileges. Older and more steady-going persons, as well as those of a higher social grade, may wish for more accommodation and a more diversified table, and so may not choose to avail themselves of the special tariff, yet if the cyclist be journeying for health or pleasure, which I take to be the true definition of touring, he will not carry any considerable quantity of luggage, and the demands on the resources of his hostelry will not differ much from those of his more rapid brother of the wheel. Everyone who uses bicycles or tricycles and who takes pleasure in wandering by road and lane may at some time or other find himself glad to take advantage of the CTC arrangements, which place at his disposal skilled assistance and intelligent comprehension of his wants. Half a crown a year can hardly be considered an ex-orbitant sum to pay for these advantages. The club last year numbered over 20,000 members.

The only obstacle that I know of to the use of the cycle becoming universal in this country, is that year by year the roads seem in many parts of England to be getting worse and worse. But, as we shall have occasion to point out further on, even in that respect there is likely to be improvement. A revolt against the present system of road repair and road surveying is being organised, and is likely to have a considerable success.

In fact, among the best of the works that have been accomplished by the two cycling organisations is the change which they are attempting in the direction of road reform. Their efforts are young as yet, and there has not been time for more than an attempt to rouse public opinion. But it has been a move in the right direction, and it is to be hoped will bear fruit ere long. No one who knows what our highways were in the coaching days can deny that roadmaking has greatly deteriorated since then. In many districts it seems to be almost a lost art. Any local busybody is considered good enough to act as road surveyor, and apparently the very last thing that occurs to those who appoint the road surveyor is the necessity of inquiring whether the candidate knows anything of road-making or not. Yet everyone must admit that it is an art, and an art that requires a considerable amount of study to acquire. Everybody is interested in having good roads, yet our highways are allowed to go from bad to worse. What is everybody's business is nobody's business, wasteful, futile, and ridiculous methods of road repair are allowed to continue, till even the tradition of good roadmaking is well nigh lost.

McAdam, the great father of our roadmaking system, used to say that no stone ought ever to be cast upon a road, for the purpose of repairing it, which could not be put in a man's mouth. The reason is obvious, small stones under the pressure of the traffic fit each other's angles, and in a short time form a mass nearly as hard as solid granite. Large stones, on the contrary, leave great gaps between their angles which hold the wet and break up the roadway, and, finally grinding upon each other, force the upper layer out above the surface. Carriage wheels are thus alternately lifted up into the air and brought down with a jerk, till the whole surface of the road is roughened. Not only is the present plan inefficacious, it is expensive as well. Twice as much material is used as would make a good roadway, and repairs have to be done very much more frequently than would be necessary if a proper system were adopted from the first.

Though the whole community are interested in the goodness of the roads, it is easy to see that the man who is dragged through ruts and over stones by the labour of his horse is not quite so keen in his appreciation of a bad road as the man who feels its effects in an aching spine and twisted muscles. So cycling roadsters, after a considerable amount of preliminary growling, have girded up their loins for action. At the beginning of 1885, or the end of 1884, a meeting was called by the Birmingham Local Centre of the NCU to discuss the question, and, if possible, devise a remedy. Somewhat to the surprise of those who called the meeting, it was attended not only by cyclists, but by horse-owners and horse-users in considerable numbers, and it was generally agreed, after lengthened deliberation, that the law was not so much at fault as the administration of it. The great difficulty was, and will no doubt continue to be, to get public opinion to bear upon a matter of rather dry detail. I venture to suggest the formation of a National Society for road reform, and I am sure that we can promise the hearty co-operation of a large body of cyclists to anyone sufficiently patriotic to set the scheme on foot. The Birmingham meeting made a small, but only a small, beginning. Eight road surveyors were summoned for neglecting to keep their roads in proper repair. The magistrates, who were informed that the prosecution was undertaken in no spirit of vindictiveness, but only to test the state of the law, eventually gave the defendants time till the second week of February in the following year, 1886, to put their roads in order. 1 have not learnt what the result of the proceeding has been, or whether the Birmingham roads are any better than they were. In any case a national movement is necessary if anything is to be done on an effective scale. Since these lines were in type the NCU have appointed a special Committee to act jointly with a similar committee of the CTC, and the joint committee have commenced active operations under the title of the 'Roads Improvement Association', which earnestly requests advice and co-operation from influential members of the two cycling institutions.

Several meetings have been held in various parts of the country, pamphlets on road repair have been circulated by the NCU and CTC, and the work is being pushed steadily ahead. With the Halesowen precedents to quote, the road surveyors in many districts are listening to the NCU requests for the improvement of the highways.

That something worth doing could be achieved if proper action were taken is proved by the following instance. In the Donington Trust road, at about the time when the old road trusts came to an end, it was found that on the highways which for the last six years of the trust had been in the skilled hands of a civil engineer instead of a non-professional road surveyor, an annual saving had been accomplished of over £267 per annum over 26 miles of road, while at the same time the roads were so much improved that a horse could draw twice as great a load as before.

It is now about four-and-twenty years since the old Turnpike Trust Acts began to expire. Sir George Grey was then at the Home Office: about the same time the formation of highway districts became permissive. Owing to that permissive character, and to the fact that the rating in unions and parishes is very unequal, only about one-third of the parishes in England are included in highway districts. From the year 1864 annual Turnpike Trust Continuance Acts have been passed. In the Bill of 1870, a clause threw the maintenance of the disturnpiked roads of which there were at that time about 1,800 miles, not upon the parishes through which they ran, but upon the highway districts, wherever such existed. The entire cost thrown upon the county rate by the Disturnpiking Act has been computed at £200,000 annually, and in many districts the highway rate has been increased threefold.

It will thus be seen that there are plenty of anomalies to be dealt with and many hardships to be redressed by the action of such a society as we have suggested.

That part of the cycling sport which relates to racing no doubt appears to assume, from its public character, a degree of importance disproportionate to the numbers of those who engage in it. Yet it is well worthy of attention, being both amusing in itself and productive of great good to the general body of cyclists who care nothing about racing. It is on the racing path where new inventions are tried, and improvements accepted.

If a new machine or a new detail for adding to the efficiency of an old one passes the fiery ordeal of the cycling experts, it is sure to come into favour with the outside cycling public within a short time. A cycling race meeting is in itself a spectacle well worth seeing. We cannot help thinking that many who know and care nothing about such meetings would, if once they attended a good one, think well of the sport they afford. The pace is good, indeed considering the distances run it may fairly be called unequalled. The best horse ever foaled would be beaten to a hopeless standstill not only by the winner, but by the last man who passes the post in a 50 miles championship race. Still more would this be the case if the race were for a distance of a hundred miles, in fact, recorded times of horses and cyclists show that after about 20 miles the horse slowly but surely falls behind.

The racing path is usually a cinder track, about a quarter of a mile in length, and square, or rather oval, in form. Owing to the high speed maintained the corners must be rounded off, even though the general shape of the ground should be square. The cinder track is carefully prepared, and on the morning of a considerable race meeting presents a beautifully firm and even surface. The distances are scrupulously measured at a distance of one foot from the inside of the track, and a small block of wood, let into the turf at the side, records the number of yards from the starting-post. These permanent marks are necessary, because at all race meetings, excepting only the annual championships, each competitor is allowed by the official handicapper of the NCU a certain number of yards start, according to the nature of his public performances. In championships all start level, and if, as is generally the case, the competitors are sufficiently numerous, the races are run in heats with seldom more than three competitors in each. The result is that in races of 5 or 10 miles the best men left in, who perhaps have to compete in two heats and a final, have to cover a great distance at top-speed before their evening's work is over. The tricycle 25 miles championship of 1885 was one of the prettiest contests ever seen. It was fought out between G. Gatehouse, of the Cambridge University Bicycle Club, and R. H. English, of the North Shields BC.

The scene of the contest was the ground of the Crystal Palace, where the track lies round the ornamental water known as the Intermediate Lake. The ground slopes sharply up from the track in all directions, making a large amphitheater of somewhat more than a quarter of a mile in diameter. On the north side nearest to the Palace are situated the grand stand and various other buildings which are used by the spectators or the competitors. A little on one side are the stands allotted to the press and the public, and further on again are the dressing-rooms in which the competitors arrange the shower-baths, rubbing-rooms, and other toilet requisites dear to the athletic mind. This description will stand with few variations for that of most of the tracks where cycling races are decided, but it is rare on this or any other path to see a contest such as that of which we are now speaking. It is not unusual for one or other of the competitors to decide on riding a waiting race. The leader not finding himself pressed, does not hurry himself – a comparative term, not inconsistent with the keeping up of a good steady pace of 18 or 19 miles an hour. The result is, or so say the public (who could not themselves go 10 miles an hour to save their lives), a slow race. But in this particular instance nothing of the kind took place. Both men started at a pace which was simply astonishing. In a few minutes, competitors, noted for their powers of speed and endurance, were left hopelessly behind by the two riders who alone, as was seen from the first, were 'in it'. Mile after mile was passed in the fastest time on record, and still the speed of these marvellous young athletes kept on undiminished. Twenty-four miles and three-quarters were thus covered, and the leaders never at any time were more than 3 yards apart. They occasionally passed each other, and in the intervals the leading man had his opponent close to his hind wheel. The spurt which the winner put on at the end of the last quarter-mile, which landed him the winner by a few yards, was a sight to be seen once in a lifetime. Mr Gatehouse has since ridden 20 miles and more – the details will be found farther on – within the hour on a tricycle; the first who has ever performed the feat, though it has been done many times on the bicycle.

I never can understand why cycle racing has not yet become more in vogue than it is among fashionable people, who are always on the look-out for some new excitement. The scene is generally a pretty one, the grounds on which the meeting is held are usually picturesquely situated, the racing is first-rate, and, unlike some other competitions of which we occasionally hear, one maybe perfectly certain that the best man will win.

It is greatly to the credit of cycling that nothing in the nature of a 'ring' has ever been allowed to be established. There is little or no betting, and there are none of the sights which make many racecourses, especially racecourses in the vicinity of towns, unfitted for the presence of ladies. They are meetings purely for sport, and if once their attractiveness was discovered, I do not doubt that they would take a very prominent place among the sports which people crowd to see.

So jealous have cyclists been as to the purity of their favourite sport, that a battle royal has been waged in recent times on the subject which no doubt has occasionally attracted the reader's attention in the newspapers, and caused him to wonder what all the disturbance was about. It is that which is known among cyclists as the 'maker's amateur' question. One of the fundamental canons of cycling law is, that no man, calling himself an amateur, may compete for a money prize, or in any way make a money profit, out of his cycling prowess. If he does, he forfeits his amateur status, and can thenceforth only race as a professional. Makers of cycling machines naturally look upon it as of great importance to have their machines ridden by the best performers, and to see them win as often as possible. To build a machine good enough to win a championship race is the best form of advertisement that could possibly occur to a maker, and he would adopt any honourable means of achieving that distinction. This is only reasonable, and indeed praiseworthy, but it came to pass in process of time that a line of conduct was adopted which, though not discreditable to the makers, who might naturally be supposed to do the best they could for their own interests, was not quite so worthy of praise when practised by racing cyclists. A class of men calling themselves amateurs and competing in amateur races, were known, or at least shrewdly suspected, to accept money from manufacturers for riding their machines. If anything of the kind was really done, it was obviously a matter very difficult to detect, and also one that was very unfair to the real amateurs who raced for a love of the sport, and for honour and glory only. The latter were at a great disadvantage, occupied during the day in business pursuits of various kinds, they were unable to give the same exclusive attention to training as those who devoted their time to it professionally. Besides, amateurs naturally wished to keep amateur races to themselves, not merely for social reasons, but because it might reasonably be supposed that persons who would race under false colours would not improbably carry their inaccuracies even farther. The result was a series of protests, an examination by a committee of the NCU, and the disqualification of a considerable number of the racing men whose names had been prominently mentioned.

Besides the amateur performers, there is, especially in the Northern and Midland counties, a considerable professional body, to whom, as to professionals in other sports, the rules about money prizes and gate-money do not apply. It is, however, remarkable that the best performances of the professionals do not except in a very few distances, exceed that of the amateurs. Cycling is not like billiards, in which professional performers are far and away in advance of all competitors. The performances of amateurs surpass at most distances those of their professional rivals, and, as a rule, at distances over 25 miles up to a hundred the record is held by amateurs.

I do not know whether any other opportunity will present itself of discussing a subject on which a considerable amount of nonsense is occasionally talked. I mean the possibility of applying electricity to tricycles. We often read that such a machine is on the point of being perfected, and there follows incontinently a great deal of quite unwarranted speculation in the newspapers as to the way in which the new adaptation of motive power will revolutionise locomotion. Fancy runs away with enthusiastic scribes, who declare that a man will be able to run from the Land's End to John o'Groat's, surmounting the most difficult hills that are encountered on the way, with an ease greater than the most accomplished cyclist can now attain to. This assumption is altogether beside the mark. The truth is that it would be quite easy to construct such a carriage, but that, as far as the ordinary cyclist is concerned, it would be absolutely useless when made. As a toy to run over a track, fitted beforehand with the necessary appliances, or between two points at which ample engine and electrical-power was available, the design of such a carriage would present no difficulty. I will produce a dozen members of the 'Dynamicable Society' who will be happy to construct one at the shortest notice. There is only one objection. It would be utterly useless when made. It would not pay. That is, for the same expense that the cost and maintenance of it would require, greatly superior modes of locomotion could be provided, whether horse or steam power that would be available for general use, instead of the extremely limited service which could be obtained from the electric machine. The limitations of which I speak depend on electrical considerations which may in future be somewhat modified but can never be entirely removed. It must be clearly understood that I am not peaking of electrical traction generally, in which I am a firm believer, and which I think is destined at no distant time to revolutionise our known modes of locomotion. I speak only of electrical traction as applied to tricycles such as are now in ordinary use.

The reasons on which these remarks are founded will be better understood if we examine the conditions on which electrical traction is possible. To make an electrical carriage travel you must have three things: (1) a motor to communicate motion to the wheels, and (2) either a dynamo or a battery of electrical storage cells popularly known as accumulators, to communicate energy to the motor, and (3) a steam engine or gas engine, to drive the dynamo, and charge the accumulators. It would be impossible in practice to carry on the tricycle itself a dynamo to impart mechanical energy to your motor, because the dynamo must itself be driven by a gas or steam engine, and if you employed either the one or the other, it would be easier, cheaper, and more economical from a mechanical point of view, to drive by steam or gas power direct, without any dynamo at all. Besides, the weight would put an engine and dynamo out of the question for a tricycle. Accumulators only need be taken into consideration.

The electrical energy to he obtained from a given accumulator is proportionate to the weight of the metal plates forming the cell. At present one of the best known and trusted forms of storage cell in the market is that known as EPS: the cell made by the Electric Power and Storage Company. I do not say it is the best. Who shall decide when doctors disagree? I am myself inclined to believe, and indeed have reason experimentally to feel convinced, that we can get a greater power in proportion to weight than is given by this cell, but in our present state of electrical knowledge the EPS is a fair cell to take as a standard. A single EPS cell is known when fully charged to give one electrical horse-power of energy for 1 hour, with a weight of between 70 and 80lb. If used at full power for an hour this cell will run down, and will have to be re-charged from a steam-engine and a dynamo before it is again used. If used at half-power the cell would last without re-charging for 2 hours, and so on in proportion.

Suppose the weight of your tricycle to be 90 lb., and a single cell, or a lot of small cells, to be 70lb, your motor and machinery could not possibly be less than 50lb, which makes up 210lb. Taking the rider at ten stone, the total weight to be driven would be at least 350 lb, and as an ordinary cyclist finds it as much as he can conveniently do to propel his own weight and a machine of 80lb, we may fairly assume that the electrical tricycle would require half a horsepower to drive it efficiently. The one horse-power of electrical energy at the rider's disposal would therefore last about 2 hours, and would then be exhausted.

For electrical reasons, it would be requisite to have more than one cell, because you could not get the full amount of efficiency out of your motor unless it was wound in such a manner as to take a current of higher tension than would be given by a single cell. But it is not necessary to go into that. I assume that one horse-power for 1 hour can be got with a weight of 70lb. If at any time the electrical energy fails, the rider will be obliged to drive by his unassisted exertion a machine of 210lb, which, as any cyclist knows, would be too much for the strength of any ordinary person. The ordinary machine weighs no more than between 8d and 90lb.

But the contingency of the electric energy failing would occur as a matter of course at the end of a couple of hours, for by that time the stored electricity would be exhausted. Unless at the end of that time the traveller was fortunate enough to find himself in the immediate neighbourhood of some person possessed of (1) a steam-engine, (2) a dynamo, and last, but not least, the accommodating disposition which would prompt him to place these advantages at the disposal of the passing cyclist, he would have to stop, or else trust to his muscles. Even if a good Samaritan with an engine and dynamo were available, the traveller's troubles would by no means be at an end, for he would have to wait while his accumulators were being re-charged. This is a long process taking 8 or 9 hours. If his 2 hour run had taken him 20 miles from home, by the time he started on his journey for another stage, he would have been 10 hours on the road, and would have travelled at the average speed of 2 miles an hour. At this rate he would take nineteen days, travelling day and night, to go from the

Land's End to John O'Groat's, and as the distance has already been performed in five days and some hours on a tricycle, and in even less time on a bicycle, the existing record time would not be broken by such a performance, and to do the journey even in nineteen or twenty days he would have to provide an engine and dynamo ready to his hand at the end of every 20 miles, which is absurd, as the great mathematician Euclid learnedly remarks in his celebrated thesis *De ponte asinorum*.

Doubtless it would be open to the owner of the electric tricycle to disregard electric horsepower, and proceed on his journey by the aid of such man-power as nature has gifted him withal, but in that case he had better discard his electric carriage, and get a lighter one. It is possible, no doubt, that in the distant future, the use of electricity may be so generally diffused that accumulators may be found everywhere available and ready charged, as a glass of beer and a crust of bread and cheese are now. It is, however, hardly worthwhile to speculate about possibilities which depend for their fulfilment on a total reversal of the present habits of the people.

As regards the construction of an electric carriage, there is really no insurmountable difficulty whatever. It is quite possible that along given lines of road electric carriages, whose arrivals and departures are carefully arranged for beforehand, may travel expeditiously and economically, but that has nothing to do with what men usually mean when they talk of electric tricycles.

It is also quite possible that even now a proprietor or manager of works where steam and electric energy are always available and constantly in use, and who has a round of 20 miles or so to make every day, might conveniently adopt an electric tricycle as a means of locomotion. In that case all the conditions of success would be at hand. After the daily round the accumulators could be recharged, but even here there is a good deal to be said in favour of a horse and a comfortable carriage behind it. The insoluble problem of an electric tricycle may be stated in a few words as follows: How to have electric energy always at hand, and always available.

Among other institutions which have been called into existence by the requirements of the cycling world, are a number of newspapers, magazines and annuals which deal almost entirely with the events and gossip of cycling life. With the exception of one or two which have a more stable existence, the newspapers die, amalgamate, and reappear in new dresses so often, that it is difficult to say with any certainty how many of them there are. In the early days, when everybody was learning to ride, and all who had taken to the wheel were busily engaged in designing new dresses, and inventing new dodges to add to the comfort of the rider, letters, editorial comments, and leaders appeared from week to week which were amusing and readable. But the best way of doing everything was at length fairly established, and it became more and more difficult from week to week to write anything new. It was a critical time for the *Cycling Press*, and it has not as yet finally discovered a way out of the difficulty. The imperative demand for 'copy' is sometimes satisfied by personalities, which are inexpressibly dreary to outsiders. Even drearier are the jokes, which refer to persons and events not generally intelligible, and are worse than the personalities. There is evidence that the leading cycling papers have been induced, by the good sense of their editors, and the opinions of the majority of their subscribers, to turn away from these defects, and revert to the healthy condition which distinguished cycling journalism when it was in the hands of a small knot of clever pioneers. As the sport spreads and cycling events of various kinds take place in all parts of the kingdom, it is increasingly difficult to supervise the lucubrations of an extended staff, but if cycling journalism is to become all that its well-wishers hope and anticipate for it, the effort must be resolutely made.

The thoughtful observer may draw for himself, from the pages of these weekly papers, a tolerably vivid picture of the social organisation which has sprung up through the intervention of cycling. The first point that suggests itself is the extent to which club life has taken possession of the younger members. Almost every village now has its cycling club, and in the towns, the accidental camaraderie afforded by a common pursuit seems to have afforded just that degree of impulse which was necessary to induce the formation and preserve the cohesion of such associations. Apart from politics as cycling necessarily is, and apart too from mere sociality, though it lends itself easily to the encouragement of social meetings of the youth of both sexes, it is difficult to find outside of cycling any inducement, operative all the year round, for the formation of clubs such as are now so common. A cricket club in January would be an absurdity, and, besides, cricket, good game as it is, does not include the gentler sex among its votaries. The reverse is the case with cycling, and anyone who will take the trouble to study the cycling papers in the winter time will see that not only do the ladies of the cycling world join in the club life to which they are by this means almost for the first time admitted, but they make their presence and influence felt in a variety of ways. In a number of a cycling paper now before me, dated on a certain winter day, there are descriptions of not one, but of half a dozen, dances given under the auspices of one or other of the well-known cycling clubs. The ladies' column, edited generally by a lady, does not omit to chronicle among other and less weighty matters the pretty toilettes which have figured at these entertainments, or to discuss with an authority to which male writers could never pretend, details of feminine cycling outfit.

Besides these dances every club has its dinners and social meetings of various kinds, and the speeches at these entertainments figure often at a considerable length in the cycling papers. It may be noted as a matter of satisfaction that, although all shades of politics must almost necessarily be represented at gatherings like these, the toasts and speeches are, without any exception that has ever come under my observation, enthusiastically loyal. The speeches naturally refer for the most part to local matters, the merits of the energetic captain of the club, the perfect amiability under provocation of the long-suffering honorary secretary, or perchance the health is proposed of some local flier who has carried off an important contest on road or path. These and trade advertisements, descriptions of mechanical improvements, or of patented nick-nacks related to cycling machines, and in some instances a well-written series of papers on mechanics, photography, or some branch of physics which might prove valuable to the cycling public, form the staple of the weekly sheets. In the number which chances to be before us the festivity fixtures occupy a whole closely printed column. There are three or four columns of editorial gossip about cycling matters, not only in this country, but also on the continent and in America. Then follow half a dozen columns of paragraphs twenty lines long giving an account of the proceedings of the more important clubs, their dinners, elections, and preparations for the next season, a balance sheet of the NCU Reserve Fund, with a stirring appeal from Major-General Christopher, a veteran who with almost boyish enthusiasm has devoted a large amount of his leisure, and his experience gained in the larger field of Indian administration, to the advancement of the interests of cycling. Then come columns devoted to the reports of 'own correspondents' in the various local centres of the NCU. There is a column devoted to inventions and inventors, and a goodly array of illustrated advertisements which shows that the circulation of the paper must suggest satisfactory reflections to the proprietors.

There is one reflection which can hardly fail to suggest itself to a recent arrival in Cyclonia, and that is the strange but undeniable fact that every third cyclist is a photographer. Perhaps photographer is too harsh a term to apply to these well-meaning persons, the justice of the case would be met in most instances by describing them as dabblers in photography. They are for the most part harmless, and operate chiefly on each other, and on their friends and relations. It is to be hoped, by those who are interested in such matters, that future generations may not be reduced to the necessity of taking their impressions of the personal appearance of the greater lights of cycling from these libellous productions. The advertising columns of the cycling papers are full of announcements of photographic materials fitted for conveyance on tricycles. The way in which cameras fold up into impossible dimensions, and so to speak almost annihilate space, is among the things no fellow can understand. I have never myself encountered one of these artists at work, but I have been told that the camera is designed to screw on to the wheel, the machine itself forming a tripod stand, and that a number of sensitive plates can be stowed away inside the backbone, or at least quite out of sight: but that perhaps is an exaggeration.

It should not be omitted while discussing the subject of cycling journalism that some of the periodicals are adorned with excellent illustrations. It is not so easy as it might seem – or if it be easy it is not often done – to draw a tricycle correctly, it need not be said that any carelessness in that respect would not be tolerated by a society of experts like those to whom the artist referred to appeals, and so his tricycles, and other cycles too, are models of correct design, and what is more, the riders of them satisfy by their correct positions on their iron steeds the strictest requirements of the most classical masters of the art. The Christmas number of *The Cyclist* for 1885, written by Messers A. J. Wilson and Morrison, and illustrated by Mr George Moore, illustrated in verse and prose, and with pen and pencil, a journey through the imaginary kingdom of Cyclonia. It was a clever squib on things and persons best known among the world of cyclists. Among notable cycling productions there should also be mentioned one which has gone through several editions, and is indeed almost, as its title indicates, indispensable to those who wish to understand the mechanism of tricycles, or to know the history of the trade – I mean Mr Henry Sturmey's *Indispensable Handbook both for the Bicycle and the Tricycle*. But the bibliography of the sport will be found elsewhere in these pages, so here I will say no more.

REST ON A RIVER BANK.

1

Historical

Cycling, in view of its recent developments, cannot be excluded from any comprehensive list of athletic sports. But at the same time it must at once be admitted that it differs in very many points from all other branches of athletics. Thus the walker, the runner, the jumper, and all other votaries of pedestrian sport, find their alpha and omega in public competitions, on the cinder path or the grass plot, and their exercises for the development of their powers, in one direction or another, are engaged in solely with a view to complete their preparation for some forthcoming contest. Although these exercises undoubtedly conduce to a healthy habit of body, sound wind, and strong, muscular limbs, yet beyond this very great gain, athletics, as such, fulfil no purpose of value to the community at large, and least of all an economic one. The cycling sport, on the other hand, has an economic side, which in real value, in its relations to everyday life, far exceeds the merely competitive developments of the pursuit, and were cycle racing, in all its branches, utterly abolished to-morrow, the interest in, and more particularly the practical value of, the sport would still continue unabated, owing to the fact that it possesses certain solid advantages which really constitute the life and soul of its particularly vigorous and healthy existence. The economic side of the sport so much insisted on may be found in the practical use of the wheel in daily life, its hygienic value as a means primarily of healthy exercise is recognised and proved by the personal and practical experiences of thousands of people throughout the world, to whom a little exercise, combined as it is with a little pleasurable and stimulating excitement, is of the very greatest value from a medical point of view. Last, but by no means least, must be considered its great convenience in the stern business of life, whether as a means of economy in time or in money. The number of clergymen who use the tricycle in the discharge of their parish duties, and find in the silent carriage, always ready at a moment's notice, the most useful and convenient of vehicles for their work, is very large, but no more need be added to what has been already said as to the economic side of the sport, as the most casual investigation will at once demonstrate clearly the growing value of the machine.

It is intended to chronicle in the following pages the past of the sport which promises to have so remarkable a future, and we may begin by remarking that the bicycle of the present day is a descendant in the right line of the 'dandy', or 'hobby horse' of 1819, so successfully and unmercifully caricatured in the facetious prints of about that date. The 'hobby horse' was a foreign introduction, having been brought from France, where its use had been almost stopped by the bitter satire and the fierce ridicule which met its users. The machine was introduced under the name of the 'Draisnene', or 'célérifére' the first name being derived from the alleged inventor, but probably only the first introducer of the hobby horse into England, who is in contemporary records called impartially Baron von Draise, Baron de Drais, M. Draise, and is said to have come from Mannheim, or from Frankfort-on-the-Main. He introduced into England from France the 'hobby horse'.

This machine consisted of two stout equal-sized wooden wheels held in iron forks, the rear fork being securely bolted to a stout bar of wood, 'the perch', while the front fork passed through the perch, and was so arranged that it could be turned by a handle, so as to steer the machine after the manner of a modern bicycle, though of course the construction was

much more clumsy and complicated. In the middle of the perch or longitudinal bar was placed a cushion, on which the rider sat, and just in front of this was another and smaller cushion raised on a bracket, on which he leaned his chest. The feet, when the rider was seated astride this contrivance, just touched the ground comfortably, and he propelled the machine by running with long and forcible strides, the machine of course progressing between the strokes and of its own accord downhill. If the contemporary sketches are any guide, this was always done at a breakneck pace, in fact, none of the earlier dandy horses had any breaks fitted to them, and, owing to their great weight, there is little doubt that they must have rushed down the hills in a somewhat startling manner. As may easily be imagined, the exercise was by no means graceful, and those who indulged in it got unmercifully laughed at, one with defining hobby-horse users as riding in their own carriages and walking in the mud at the same time. A glance at the caricatures of the period, of which there is a good collection in the British Museum, will show to what an extent the novel exercise must have been taken up. In one graphic sketch the blacksmiths ol a posting village are seen pursuing the hobby riders, upsetting them and smashing their machines to pieces with hammers, the inscription showing that this was done because the hobby never required shoeing, while a glance at a genuine hobby, several good specimens of which exist, demonstrates the fact that, unlike their successors of 1895, the blacksmiths of 1819 could hardly have earned anything for the repair of breakdowns, the sturdy proportions of the machine looking as if they would defy all attempts to injure it, albeit the spectator naturally wonders what would have been the fate of an unfortunate rider who got mixed up with the clumsy and heavy vehicle in the case of a fall. Unmercifully lampooned and ridiculed, the beaux and dandies of the day soon dropped this somewhat laborious exercise, and the hobby disappeared almost entirely from public view. A few yet remained, and were ridden by a small body of enthusiasts who still hoped to popularise the sport. But the jar of the iron-tired wheels, and the peculiarly awrkward position (which tended to produce hernia), soon obtained for the machine a very bad name, and its use gradually lapsed. Still, eleven years after the great hobby year of 1819, namely in 1830, it is recorded that certain 'improved dandy horses' were issued to the postmen in a rural district, where, doubtless, they were used for many years, but they were not replaced as they wore out, and the postmen had once again to trudge on foot.

It was not until two or three years prior to the Great Exhibition of 1862 that the first real advance is recorded towards the production of the bicycle of today. Velocipedes or carriages to go without horses, manivelociters, four bivectors, one trivector, accelerators, allepode', had one after another been brought before the public, as the latest and most valuable invention in this direction. Some of the designs were marvellous in their impracticability. One, for example, was a full-sized coach with accommodation for six persons, one of whom steered from the box, four passengers sat inside, and the whole was to be driven by means of two foot levers by one footman, who was to stand in full uniform at the back of the coach as footmen usually do. This unfortunate is represented in a three-cornered hat and a laced coat, and cyclists of today will doubtless be ready to sympathise with the unfortunate persons who were called upon to attempt this light and easy task. A glance at some of the scientific journals of the time will show that in the early days of velocipedes inventors were as enthusiastic, in their belief in their designs, as the most impracticable of modern geniuses. Our manufacturers claim for the machines they make the highest qualities of lightness, strength and speed, ignoring the fact that the last named qualification depends upon the man, and not on the machine he rides. Inventors nowadays invariably pooh-pooh opposition, and assert the great advantages possessed by their last invention, and so, we find, did their prototypes before the bicycle was invented. Thus the following appears in No. 57 of mechanics' magazine, museum, register, journal, and gazette, published on Saturday 25 September 1824:

Mr D. McDonald, of Sunderland, informs us that he has invented a 'self-moving machine' for travelling on roads, which has carried seven persons. It is propelled by means of treadles. A man sits behind working the same, and there is a fly-wheel operating upon two cog-wheels, which operate on a square axle. You will, perhaps, think the man behind has hard labour – not so. From the velocity of the fly-wheel, together with the aid of a lever, which is in the hand of a person in front steering, he has not often to put his feet to the treadles. Mr McDonald intends, when he shall have improved the friction of the body of the carriage, to present the same to the Society of Arts, and as he desires to receive no emolument for the same, he hopes it will come into general use.

How charming was the confidence, how great the magnanimity, of Mr McDonald! Perchance he 'improved the friction of the body of the carriage' too much, for, strange to say, it never seems to have come into the general use anticipated by its inventor. 'You will perhaps think the man behind has hard labour?' Perhaps! With seven persons in the 'self-moving' carriage it would have been doubly interesting to have heard the sentiments of 'the man behind'. In the same magazine, in its issue for 6 September of the same year, there is a record of another of these facetiously named 'self-moving carriages', invented by a carpenter of Buckland, near Chard, which is said to have been of 'very light construction', while K. W., a Welshman, describes a lever-action machine, which accommodated two persons besides 'the one who conducted it', and it is further stated by its inventor that it 'went, with ease, 8 mph'. This must have been under favourable circumstances, say down a very steep hill, for a steep hill only would have sufficed to overcome the friction of the numerous cogs and chains introduced into the Welshman's design. All the 'self-moving carriages' of this early date were to be propelled by levers, but there seems every probability that the credit of first applying the crank action to velocipedes belongs to an English firm, as Messers Mehew of Chelsea showed in the Exhibition of 1862 a three-wheeled velocipede, the front wheel steering as in a modern bicycle or the old dandy horse, the other two wheels, which were of course somewhat smaller, being placed side by side behind. This type is to be seen today in children's toy tricycles, and also at the Crystal Palace and other places where velocipedes are let out on hire by the hour. This English-made machine was fitted with a pair of cranks to the front wheel.

The hobby horse of forty years before was not forgotten, and it is more than probable that several of the visitors conceived the idea of fitting the cranks to the dandy horse from seeing the Chelsea firm's velocipede at the Exhibition, albeit there is pretty good evidence forthcoming to prove that the crank had been so adapted previously to 1862. Gavin Dalzell, a cooper of Lesmahagow, Lanarkshire, was for a long time given the credit of being the first user of a crank-driven bicycle, but after an exhaustive investigation Mr James Johnson of Glasgow has been able to establish the fact that Kirkpatrick Macmillan, of Courthill, Keir near Penpont, Dumfriesshire, rode such a machine between 1830 and 1840. The cranks were fitted to the rear wheel, and long bars were attached to them and jointed to swinging levers in front. About 1866, a Parisian firm, M. M. Michaux et Cie., sent over to England a perfected bicycle, which was considered at that time the acme of ingenuity and lightness – it is scarcely necessary to add that the same machine would nowadays excite amusement and derision by its weight and clumsiness. The first machines imported found their way to the gymnasiums, and one of the earliest arrived, in January 1869, at a gymnasium conducted by Mr Charles Spencer, who was destined to do much towards the introduction of a sport which has now taken so great a hold upon the public favour. The account which is given in an old magazine of the arrival of this machine may be briefly epitomised as follows:

In the early part of January 1869 [writes 'John M.'], who may now be identified with Mr John Mayall, the photographer of Regent Street] I was at Spencer's Gymnasium in Old Street, St Luke's ... when a foreign-looking packing-case was brought in ... As the case was opened I recognised a piece of apparatus consisting mainly of two wheels, similar to one I had seen not long before in Paris, but the one I saw in Paris was much smaller, and a lad being mounted upon it who drove the machine by putting his feet easily to the ground, I looked upon it as a mere *jouet d'enfant* such as the Parisians are so clever in designing. It produced but little impression on me, and certainly did not strike me as being a new means of locomotion. A slender young man, whom I soon came to know as Mr Turner of Paris, followed the packing-case and superintended its opening, the gymnasium was cleared, Mr Turner took off his coat, grasped the handles of the machine, and with a short run, to my intense surprise, vaulted on to it, and, putting his feet on the treadles, made the circuit of the room. We were some half-dozen spectators, and I shall never forget our astonishment at the sight of Mr Turner whirling himself round the room, sitting on a bar above a pair of wheels in a line that ought, as we innocently supposed, to fall down immediately he jumped off the ground. Judge then of our greater surprise when, instead of stopping by tilting over on one foot, he slowly halted, and turning the front wheel diagonally, remained quite still, balancing on the wheels.

'John M.'s' experiences are curious as illustrating the fact which so few can realise nowadays, that at that time the possibility of remaining on two wheels arranged bicycle-wise was not recognised. This writer's ideas of riding at this early stage were confined to a conviction that he must hold the handle straight, in a most unyielding manner, but he soon mastered the machine sufficiently to ride from London to Red Hill, in an attempt to get to Brighton, and he returned from Red Hill by train, exhausted and covered with dust and glory.

Such, then, was the advent of the bicycle. These earlier machines were of great weight, a radical fault which speedily began to be corrected, the riders of the machine, even at this early period, having a very clear appreciation of the value of lightness in the vehicles they had to propel. English manufacturers very soon began to take up the business, and, with characteristic thoroughness, went in for improvements from the first. Capital was invested, plant laid down, and a rapid change took place. The French vehicles, light as they were by comparison with the old velocipedes and dandy horses, were soon surpassed by the English-made goods. The French machines were indeed regarded merely as toys, and the manufacturers, with the experiences of the dandy horse before them, thought that the new fancy would die out as rapidly as did the earlier one, but their English confreres with greater perspicuity saw that the new machine had a great future before it, and made their arrangements accordingly.

The earliest enterprises of note in connection with the manufacture of cycles were started in Coventry. The trade in woollen and worsted stuffs of this city and of the county of Warwickshire was at one time very extensive, but it gradually decreased owing to the establishment of an important branch of the ribbon trade, employing at one time 17,000 or 18,000 looms. This latter branch of industry had in turn been much depressed, partly through foreign competition, and other branches of business were similarly affected. The city was therefore eager to welcome a new enterprise, the manufacture of the bicycle was taken up, and Coventry soon became noted for the excellent machines which were despatched from its workshops. 'The city of spires', as Coventry is called, thus became the metropolis of the cycling trade, and the centre from which thousands of the best machines are distributed annually throughout the civilised world, and, as a natural sequence, the headquarters of the largest and most widely circulated of the many papers devoted to the interests of the sport, *The Cyclist*. The three and four wheeled velocipedes of a former day fell rapidly into disuse, and the light and speedy two-wheeler grew as quickly in public favour. The bicycle was soon encountered in every part of the kingdom. Many a good story is told of its first appearances in out-of-the-way places. *Punch*'s benighted countryman, bolting from an apparition which 'looked like a man a-ridin upon nawthin', illustrated but one phase of the astonishment with which people regarded the novelty. The growth of the sport in public favour was very rapid, and cautious observers again began to remind manufacturers and cyclists of the fate of the hobby horse, and to prognosticate the early fall of the bicycle from its mushroom elevation, but, just at this time, when a slight lull in the interest occurred, the records of several feats of long-distance road-riding found their way into the papers, and at once opened the eyes of the public to the fact that the toy of the hour possessed solid advantages which would insure for it a permanent place among the pastimes of the age. A machine, of whatever type, which would enable a man to ride 40, 50, or even 60 miles in a day, with comparative ease and comfort, must, the observers argued, be of some service, and accordingly everyday brought fresh pupils to the cycling teachers to acquire a practical acquaintance with, and take an active part in, the new sport.

In the meantime the makers were by no means idle, and various modifications of the original machine were rapidly introduced. Wooden wheels and solid iron frames were replaced by 'spider' or suspension wheels constructed entirely of metal and tubes of the same material. India-rubber superseded the iron tires, and improvement after improvement was devised until the invention of the step made it possible to mount still higher wheels.

Many ingenious mechanics laboured at this time in the field of cycling invention, prominent among them was Mr James Starley. Keen of apprehension, fertile in expedients, Mr Starley had settled down in the employ of the Coventry Machinist Company, then devoted to the manufacture of several classes of sewing machines, the trade having been encouraged in Coventry to find employment for a number of persons hitherto engaged in the watch trade, which was then at a very low ebb. As far back as 1865 Starley had made avelocipede with suspension wheels. It was not so marked a success as to encourage him to persevere in that direction, but in 1868 he saw a bicycle for the first time, a French-made machine having been brought to Coventry by a nephew of Mr J. Turner, the manager of the Coventry Machinist Company. This gentleman, Mr Rowley Turner, is probably identical with the 'Mr Turner, of Paris', who took a velocipede to Spencer's gymnasium. Mr Turner was anxious to place an order for a number of these machines, and the manager of the company happily accepted it. Thenceforward the cycle-manufacturing trade grew rapidly, and many hundreds of firms in all parts of the kingdom are now engaged in producing cycles and their accessories, Coventry, Birmingham and Nottingham being perhaps the most important centres of the business.

Competition is very keen, and the result is that each maker tries to excel the others in some way. One firm makes a speciality of one class of machine, another of another, and in all cases the result is of direct benefit to the active cyclist, for any point which requires attention is instantly looked into by ingenious and clever mechanics, and a remedy or improvement suggested. To those who have not carefully investigated the matter the price paid for machines seems high, but it must be remembered that before the cycle can be brought to the necessary pitch of excellence a vast amount of money has to be spent in experiments, and any small item of alteration or improvement may throw out of use machines or parts which lie ready to hand. Thus the manufacturer is constantly finding himself burdened with obsolete patterns in castings and machines which, but a few weeks before, represented the 'latest improvements'. Moreover, the skill employed in the construction of a trustworthy machine has to be paid for, and paid for highly. Skill has much to do with it. It is perfectly well known that two workmen may be working side by side with the same materials, and that one will make a wheel which may last ten years, while the other may make one which will not stay true for ten days. The exact reason is difficult to discover and as no test but a practical one is of any service in these cases it will be easily understood that the services of a good workman are not to be obtained for nothing, while a visit to any large cycle works will show that many machines and much skill and ingenuity have to be exercised before the modern machine can be placed satisfactorily on the market.

A trade thus rapidly developing necessarily implied a steady and increasing demand for its productions, and that demand could only be legitimately fostered and encouraged by the performance of some noteworthy feats upon the newly introduced machine. In the earlier days of the sport these took the form of long rides upon the roads. One of the first of such performances was a trip undertaken by certain members of the Middlesex BC from London to John O' Groat's House, the most northern point of the British Isles. The four tourists were Messers C. Spencer, Hunt, Leaver, and Wood, and the ride was begun on 2 June 1873. The machines were of the most approved type, although of course very unlike the vehicles of today. The four adventurous riders were accompanied for a few miles of their way by friends, but they soon distanced their escort, and, pressing on, reached Buckden in the evening, having rather injudiciously ridden 65 miles in the first day, this being a very notable performance at that period. On 3 June the party rode on, and, after encountering a rustic who upset one of their number, they eventually reached Newark, the second day's journey being 43 miles. On the 4th, Wentbridge was reached, the distance covered being 47 miles. June 5 proved wet and windy, and the wayfarers suffered accordingly, only accomplishing 23 miles, and reaching Wetherby very much exhausted. 6 June was more favourable, and the party covered 47 miles ere resting for the night at Darlington. On the 7th Newcastle was reached, distance for the day 32 miles; 8th, Alnwick, 34 miles; 9th, Dunbar: the roads and weather being very favourable, the riders went 55 miles; 10th, Edinburgh only, in very bad weather, 28 miles; 11th, Birmingham, a journey of 70 miles, some part of it however being represented by the ferry across the Firth of Forth, 12th, Kingussie, a good ride of 60 miles; 13th, Moy Inn, 40 miles; 14th, Dingwall, a distance of 23 miles; 15th, Helmsdale, 17 miles, and on the 16th, fifteen days from the start, the party reached John O' Groat's House, and thus brought to a conclusion the first long-distance road ride on record. This of course attracted a great deal of attention at the time, and did much to bring home to the observant public the real value and capabilities of the bicycle.

In 1869 Mr Mayall, after his early experiences with the bicycle, determined to ride to Brighton, and this he did on 17 February of that year. He started in company with some friends, but was the only one of the party who accomplished the feat. He reached the popular watering-place in about 12 hours, and it may be noted, as an illustration of the improved pace now achieved, that Mr C. G. Wridgway went there and back in a few minutes more than five and a half hours.

Some notable distance rides were also accomplished by C. A. Booth, F. V. T. Honeywell, J. H. Palmer, C. Mansell, G. Croft, and others.

The interest excited by the road rides was soon diverted into parallel channels, and bicycle racing became a popular branch of the sport, the public evincing great interest in the new form of athletic exercise. Early in 1869 some cycling races were held at the Crystal Palace on the top terrace (the paved one), on which the Sphinxes stand, the races being straight away, without a turn, while inside the Palace a velocipede show was held, in which were exhibited some wonderful manu-motive carriages, notable among them being an eight-oared boat, mounted on wheels, and propelled by levers arranged to represent oars, the coxswain sitting at the stern of the boat and steering with straps which passed to the bow, so anxious were its inventors to maintain the aquatic parallel. On the same occasion some sports took place, riders in fancy costumes tilting at the ring and the quintain in front of the Handel Orchestra.

This description of entertainment, however, soon gave way to the more legitimate forms of racing, and meetings were held in the Agricultural Hall at Islington, and also at Nottingham, Wolverhampton, and elsewhere.

From 1869 until today the sport of cycle racing has continued to increase in popular favour with only one slight check in 1883, when interest somewhat waned, only to become all the stronger in 1884. The inclusion of cycling races in the programs of athletic sports has increased the popularity of those gatherings to a marked extent, and the rapid spread of cycling has of course been much encouraged by the public performances of the racing men.

Thousands of followers of the sport first had their interest aroused by the performances of our leading path riders, noticeably by the deeds accomplished by John Keen during the time he held championship honours or shared them with F. Cooper, and also by the fine riding of the late H. L. Cortis. When that splendid cyclist first accomplished the feat, on which he had so long set his heart, of riding 20 miles in the hour, the fact was widely commented on in the public press, and of necessity drew the attention of many an outsider to the sport.

In the earlier days the doctors were very much opposed to cycling, a prejudice having arisen against it owing to the fact that the jerks and jars of the original boneshaker induced headache and sometimes hernia, which latter result was very common among constant users of the original hobby horse, but ere long many of them saw reason to modify their prejudices against the bicycle. It was not, however, until the advent of the perfected tricycle that the faculty gave their support with anything like unanimity to cycling, but when the tricycle was sufficiently perfected, a large number of medical men adopted it for their own use, and very soon saw that the sport possessed special advantages from a merely health-giving point of view. Many a business man has found that the use of the tricycle combines healthy exertion with a certain amount of excitement and novelty, an amusement which affords the necessary exercise without being monotonous, and many instances could be quoted of its value in this connection. One will perhaps suffice. A medical man through ill health occasioned by an accident suffered from headache and nervousness, could not bear to sit in either a carriage or a railway train, and often walked long distances to avoid the dreaded methods of conveyance. One day at a friend's house he saw a tricycle, and becoming interested he ventured to try it. The exercise pleased him. He investigated the details of the machine and occasionally rode it, and one day awoke to the fact that he had covered 10 miles without suffering, although his common sense told him that there was more jar about it than there would be in either a railway train or a carriage. Confidence thus established, he purchased a machine and rode continuously, his nervous affection was quite overcome, his own remark being that he was so concerned to know whether he was going to run over a chance half-brick in the road that he quite forgot that his head ought to beaching, and he eventually was able to subdue the trouble which threatened seriously to interfere with his comfort in life. This is but one of the many instances which might be quoted of the special value which the tricycle more particularly possesses in such cases. The novelty, mild excitement, and gentle exercise, all combine to make the pursuit so fascinating that the rider becomes expert while interest in the new pastime is fresh, and then, being expert, finds new pleasures in the pursuit.

The popularity of the new vehicle continued to increase while its economic capabilities were also fully recognised by the press. In the issue of the *Daily News* for 23 August 1876, there was a leader upon the bicycle, pointing out its various advantages, and emphatically endorsing its claim to notice. It contained *inter alia* the assertion that the bicycle 'ought to be regarded not as a mere plaything of the hour, but as a substantial addition to the conveniences of life.' A considerable advance this upon the 'Jouet d'Enfant', from Paris!

On 2 September 1876, Messers Frank Smytheand W. E. N. Coston (the latter afterwards became a celebrated amateur walker) rode 205 miles in 22 hours on the road, the actual time in the saddle being 17 hours 17 minutes. This feat eclipsed Mr H. S. Thorp's ride from London to York in 22.5 hours, the distance being 195.5 miles, which may be amusingly compared with the following announcement, a copy of which is still preserved at the 'Black Swan' at York:

All that are desirous to pass from London to York, or from York to London, or any other place on that road, let them repair to the Black Swan in Holbourne, London, and to the Black Swan in Coney Street, York, at each which places they may be received in a stage coach every Monday, Wednesday, and Friday, which performs the whole journey in four days, if God permits.

'York Four Days Coach begins the 18th April, 1703'

Rides like these naturally attracted much attention, but unhappily, then as now, there existed a number of evil-disposed persons who seemed to imagine that the bicycle had no right upon the roads, and who constantly seized every opportunity of hampering and interfering with any cyclists they chanced to meet. One very flagrant case occurred on Saturday 26 August 1876, when the driver of the St Albans coach lashed, with his whip, a bicyclist who was passing, while the guard, who had provided himself beforehand with an iron ball on the end of a rope, threw it between the spokes of the machine and dragged it and the rider to the ground. The driver was fined £2 for the assault, and also paid the rider £10 towards the damage to his machine, while the guard was fined £5. As an outcome of this case 'a protection society for cyclists', the embryo NCU, was discussed at some length in the contemporary press, but without producing any immediate result. The popularity which the little Surrey village of Ripley and its neighbourhood now enjoys (thousands of cyclists being accustomed to visit the place on holidays and such-like occasions) renders the following extract from a journal published in October 1876 very amusing: 'As some proof of the hold bicycling is taking as an exercise' writes the editor, 'despite the fearful state of the roads and sky overhead, no less than thirteen men rode to Ripley and dined there on Sunday last, including two of the racers at the Oval on the previous day.'

On 9 October John Keen, the then almost invincible professional champion, rode 50 miles in 3 hours, 6 minutes; 45 seconds, which was at that time a best on record. No fewer than 102 race meetings were held in 1876, which demonstrates clearly the advance made, amounting to an increase of just 50 per cent, beyond the previous year, and the season closed with a marked increase in the number of cyclists and in the interest taken by the general public in the new branch of athletic sport.

In 1877 the rivalry between John Keen and Fred Cooper ran high. The pair contested frequent races for the One Mile Professional Championship, and one athletic paper grumbled because '12,000 people attended a Wolverhampton meeting to see two men ride a mile' – a somewhat amusing commentary on the rapid spread of the sport which had but a few months back been superciliously patronised by the athletic section. W. Tomes of the Portsmouth Club succeeded, in April 1877, in beating the One-Mile bicycle record by no less than five seconds, his record, which was, however, soon eclipsed, standing at 3 minute and 5 seconds. The *West Sussex Gazette*, one of the largest provincial newspapers, was much taken to task for its assertion that 60,000 machines were in use at this time in the United Kingdom, and the calculation does appear somewhat excessive for 1877. On 7 September of this year the *Daily Telegraph* in the course of a leader, said, 'Bicycling is a healthy and manly pursuit with much to recommend it, and unlike many foolish crazes, it has not died out,' and during the following week the West Kent BC held a race meeting on the terrace of the Crystal Palace, Sydenham, at which the late Lord Sherbrooke presented the prizes to the successful competitors. In the course of his remarks he praised the bicycle as a pleasing and healthful method of recreation, and claimed to have ridden a dandy horse in the reign of George IV. Lord Sherbrooke differed, as will be gathered, from the editor of the *Percy Anecdotes*, for he speaks of the Marquess of Worcester, who lived in the sixteenth century, as having suggested 'that foolish thing of modern – though now almost obsolete – use, the velocipede'. In this year, on the August Bank Holiday, the first meet at Harrogate was held, the Cyclists' Camp, which afterwards became so popular, being still in the clouds. The Amateur Championship of the year fell to Mr Wadham Wyndham, of the London BC

Even at this early date the cyclists were complaining of the position assumed towards the sport by the athletic associations and clubs, energetic protests were made, and cyclists were urged to combine to promote their own championship contests in place of the A. A. C. competition 'with its half-guinea entrance fee and half-guinea medal.'

Mr Wyndham's was the last contested A. A. C. Championship, as, after two walks over, the race was finally dropped in favour of the championships then started and since carried on by the NCU, first established as the Bicycle Union in 1878. Meets also helped to draw public attention to the sport. A great gathering of riders was annually organised at Hampton Court. Mustering in Sandy Lane or on the Green, the riders started in a procession in pairs, each club being headed by its captain, and rode round a course previously set forth, some 4 to 5 miles in extent, ending at the top of the Chestnut Avenue, Bushey Park, this the riders passed down, and, going to right and left of the Diana Fountain, rode out through the double gates and dismounted. The press and the public took much interest in the demonstration, which, at its best, attracted some 2,000 riders, and the sport and trade received a valuable fillip just at the right time of the year.

Judged by the light of subsequent events, 16 June was a red-letter day in the history of cycling, as on that date the late Mr H. L. Cortis, of the Wanderers BC, made his debut at a private meeting of his own club, held in the grounds of the Caterham Asylum, where the future champion at all distances ran second in a 1 mile handicap, with 100 yards start, and first in a 5 mile handicap with 350 yards start, the scratch man being Mr A. P. C. Percival.

The *Cycling Press* was now crowded with letters suggesting the formation of unions, associations, or leagues, for the furtherance and development of bicycling, and letters appeared weekly in support of various plans for the consolidation and organisation of the cycling interests, with results which will be found duly set forth in the chapters devoted to the NCU and the CTC, those great associations of which cycling is so justly proud. In this year the proprietors of *The Sporting Life* placed in the hands of the proprietor of Lillie Bridge Grounds (as representing the Amateur Athletic Club, which was at that time promoting the Four Miles Amateur Championship of Cycling) a 50 guinea cup, to be run for over a distance of 50 miles, under the title of 'The Sporting Life' Cup. This gift was duly announced to the cycling world, and was first competed for on 27 October, when it was won by Mr Harry Osborne of the Surrey BC after a very fine race. The cup was put up annually for a time after this first contest, but the assumption by the AAC of the Four Miles Championship as the championship, and the subsequent claim that this cup represented the Fifty Miles Championship, clashed unsuccessfully with the claims of the Fifty Miles Championship established by the Bicycle Union, and caused loyal supporters of the latter body to oppose the event. It ultimately collapsed, and nothing has been heard of the cup since 1883.

1877 had shown a steady advance in the position of the sport. New clubs had been formed, more races run, and generally more interest awakened. The makers were reaping the natural results of increased demand, and everything presaged a good cycling season in 1878. Early in that year a good deal of fun was made out of the fact that, at the annual meeting of the Society for Promoting the Employment of Additional Curates, the Bishop of Manchester stated that he understood a brother bishop had suggested the use of the bicycle to curates in his diocese, the Bishop of Carlisle, following in the same strain, regretting the hilliness of the country where he held sway, and facetiously remarking that if there was one thing a bicycle objected to, it was going uphill. The bishops could not foresee the practical use that would be made of the cycle by hundreds of the clergy throughout the length and breadth of the land today.

On 10 June 1878, Mr F. E. Appleyard made his magnificent record between Bath and London in the London BC 100 Miles Road Race, his time being 7 hours, 18 minutes; 55 seconds and his actual time in the saddle but 6 hours, 38 minutes; 55 seconds, a splendid performance, especially as for many miles towards the end of the journey the rider suffered severely from cramp, and on one or two occasions had to dismount as the pain was so great. Appleyard scarcely did anything afterwards, but his record was left undisturbed until 1884. On the day on which Mr Appleyard performed this feat another very well-known rider, who still takes an active interest in cycling, Mr G. Pembroke Coleman, traversed the 100 miles in 7 hours, 25 minutes; 20 seconds, finishing third, Mr W. T. Thorn, the well-known racing man, being second. Mr Coleman's performance stamps him as a sound and practical exponent of a sport in which he holds so important an office.

In this year the tricycle was first really advertised as a practical vehicle. Messers Haynes & Jeffries, of the Ariel Works, announced the 'New Patent Coventry Tricycle', which had been invented for the firm by James Starley. Several tricyclists can remember their first essays on this, one of the earliest and best machines obtainable before the introduction of the balance gear. Long rides again marked the close of an important season. W. Britten, of the Clarence BC, rode from the Marble Arch to Bath and back, 212 miles, within 24 hours on 12 September, and in the same month Mr Smythe, who rode with Mr W. E. N. Coston in a similar attempt some time before, again essayed the 24 hours road record on the Wisbech Road, and covered 218 miles, but as he picked his ground, and simply traversed it over and over again, the performance cannot compare with that accomplished by the captain of the Clarence. On the 13th, the day after Mr Britten's feat, Mr W. T. Thorn, the London BC racing man, made a bold and nearly successful attempt to ride from London to York in the 24 hours. He succeeded in reaching Doncaster, 162 miles, in 17 hours and 10 minutes, having thus 6 hours, 50 minutes, in hand in which to cover the remaining 35 miles, and he felt both well and confident of accomplishing the feat with nearly two hours to spare, when the felloe of his wheel unfortunately broke under him, thus destroying his chance of putting on a record which would have stood nearly as long as Appleyard's 100 miles.

On September 5 an event occurred which drew a vast amount of attention to the bicycle. *The Times* on that date published an appreciative leader upon the new vehicle, containing the following remarks upon the steel steed:

The bicycle has come to the front, and is fighting for existence. Dimly prefigured in the mythical centaur, and then in the hobby horse of mediaeval games, and attempted in the velocipede, now half a century old, long prejudiced by the evident superiority of wings to wheels, the bicycle has now surmounted the difficulties of construction, and adapted itself to human capabilities – it augments at least threefold the locomotive power of an ordinary man. A bicyclist can perform a journey of 100 miles in one day with less fatigue than he could walk 30, 50 miles – that is, from London to Brighton – as easily as he could walk ten, and a daily journey to and fro between London and the distant suburbs with just the usual results of moderate exercise.

After alluding to possible ills which might arise from indulgence in the sport, the writer states,

Bicyclists are aware they run dangers, and suffer a percentage of casualties, but they have counted the cost and found it worthwhile running the risk. From other points of view the objections are loud and numerous, but have upon the whole a striking family resemblance to many former objections, such, for example, as those made at the introduction of railways. The chief objection re-appears in great force.

Horses, it must be admitted, do not like bicycles, but neither do they like railways, and they will probably like street locomotives still less.

Going at length into the question of the dangers to the public arising from the use of the bicycle in the public streets, the writer winds up an essentially favourable article by saying,

The Legislature would be very unfaithful to the courageous principals which have hitherto guided it in the treatment of discoveries and improvements if it showed any prejudice in this matter. That would be a great injustice to the men, most of them still young, who have won for themselves a great convenience, and no less pleasure, at no cost whatever, it may be said, and without drawing upon the common fund of the food of man. Society used to be divided into the equestrian and the pedestrian orders, these people have found a third rank. Their success proves, as Johnson says, what man can do.

The closing event of 1878 was the practical retirement from the Presidency of the Bicycle Union of Mr G. F. Cobb, who had undoubtedly been the means of establishing that body upon a firm basis, and of arranging the conditions under which it has since become so marked a success.

1879 was destined to see a still further spread in the popularity of the sport and the initiation of many new votaries into its mysteries. Early in the year the now celebrated Surbiton path, upon which the late Mr H. L. Cortis did several of his finest performances, was thrown open to the public, and found much favour. Its fastest rival, the Cambridge track, was the scene of some further alterations of the record table, as on 21 May Mr Fred T. East, of the Surrey BC, won the University Ten Miles Invitation Race in 30 minutes, 45 seconds, when a best on record, and on the same occasion by special permission a mixed contest between amateurs and professionals was held, the distance being 2 miles. The selected riders were John Keen and Fred Cooper for the professionals, and the Hon. Ion Keith-Falconer and Mr H. L. Cortis for the amateurs. The race was a very remarkable one. Cortis dashed off from the start at a rapid pace, closely followed by Keen, Keith-Falconer, and Cooper, in the order named, and these positions were maintained up to the three-quarter mile post. Cooper, who was essentially a sprinter, waited until 200 yards from the completion of the half distance, and then dashed away, leading the quartette by some yards at the mile, reached in 2 minutes, 47 seconds, best on record. Keith-Falconer dashed after Cooper, with Keen on his hind wheel, and Cortis was left a yard or two in the rear. In this order they covered 1.5 miles. Still keeping in front, Falconer stalled off a tremendous spurt on Keen's part, and won by about 3 inches in the marvellous time of 5 minutes, 36 seconds. If any evidence was wanted of the extraordinary nature of the feat, it is to be found in the length of time it stood in the record books, as it was not till the autumn of 1884, more than five years after it had been accomplished, that the flying Tynesider, R. H. English of the North Shields Club, beat these figures by covering 2 miles in the race for the Fifteen Miles Crystal Palace Challenge Cup in 5 minutes, 333 seconds. English's record was defeated after but a short existence by Webber who, on the Cambridge track in the Two Miles Invitation Race in which he defeated W. A. Ulston, covered the distance in 5 minutes, 30 seconds.

On June 28, at a race meeting promoted by the Druids BC, G. Lacy Hillier made his first appearance on a London cinder path (his debut having been made on the gravel track at the Alexandra Palace). At Lillie Bridge, in the One Mile Handicap, receiving 155 yards start from Cortis, after winning his heat he ran into the fence at the grandstand end of the track and fell. He was unplaced in the final.

In August yet another record was established between London and John O' Groat's, H. Blackwell, of the Canonbury BC having covered the distance in 11 days and 4 hours, arriving at John O' Groat's house on 27 August. In September the Surrey BC offered for the first time a fifty-guinea cup, to be won three times in all, for competition in their scratch race, distance 10 miles, and H. L. Cortis placed his name upon it, making a best on record for 10 miles on grass – 34 minutes and 31.5 seconds. The tricycle had now begun to make its way steadily in public opinion, and as a result a Kensington agent decided to promote a 50 miles road race, the course being from Kew Bridge to Blackwater and back. The winner turned up in A. E. Derkinderin, who covered the distance in 4 hours and 55 minutes. This race was carried on from year to year by a committee, until it was stopped by the police, near Caterham Junction, as a nuisance.

In October Cortis did the Alexandra Palace managers a good turn, as on the old path, which was by no means in good condition, the 'Long Wanderer', as Cortis was called, made a 3 miles record, covering that distance in the final of the Three Miles Open Handicap in 8 minutes and 55 seconds. All who saw the race must remember how the white-vested athlete flew down and up the hill and dashed at top speed round the, then unbanked, lower corner, while the last lap was a magnificent effort, and the victor well deserved the cheers which welcomed his return to the dressing room.

The celebrated Over Turnpike case, in which the gatekeepers were fined for demanding an exorbitant toll, 5s, from a bicyclist, upsetting him and detaining his lamp because he would not pay it, was decided about this time in favour of the rider, and the decision encouraged the cycling fraternity considerably.

The Cortis-Keen matches, which created such a sensation at the time, were run off in 1879. Much discussion had taken place in cycling circles as to the relative merits of the acknowledged champions of professional and amateur cycling. Keen possessed fine speed, and his judgment was far more matured than that of Cortis, who the next year lost the mile championship through want of 'head.' The union showed its real strength by granting a permit for a series of contests at 1, 5, and 20 miles, and as Keen's old friends in Wolverhampton of course wished to see him ride, the 20 mile race was run there. The idea that the amateur had a ghost of a chance with the professional was scouted by the habitues of the Molyneux Grounds. The professional adopted waiting tactics, and Cortis made all the running at a good pace. Three hundred yards from home Keen made a tremendous effort, but the amateur won handsomely by 3 yards. Times: 5 miles, 16 minutes, 10 seconds; 10 miles, 32 minutes, 115 seconds; 15 miles, 48 minutes, 19 seconds; 20 miles, 64 minutes, 43 seconds. Keen rode a 56-inch and Cortis a 60-inch 'Keen's Eclipse' bicycle.

The 1 and 5 mile races were run off at Stamford bridge. Keen had been taking much care of himself after his Wolverhampton experiences, while Cortis had without doubt been made anxious by the over-solicitous attentions of his friends, and he was conspicuously nervous on coming to the mark. Keen, inured by a larger experience, was by far the cooler of the two, and as usual was content to wait. Cortis cut out the running in the mile at a fair pace, and no change occurred until rounding the corner into the straight for home, when Keen drew up and going wide spurted in marvelous form. Cortis, probably from over-anxiety, seemed to go to pieces, and was very erratic in his steering, and suffered defeat by a foot. Time: 2 minutes and 52 seconds. This result upset Cortis altogether, and in the 5 miles (in which his only chance lay in forcing the pace) he sat up to make Keen lead at $1^{1/2}$ miles. Keen being forced to the front only crawled round, and Cortis in disgust did what he should have done at first and spurted marvellously. When the bell rang Cortis went for the last lap but Keen, timing his effort to a nicety, won by a yard.

Cortis was dreadfully upset at his defeat, but it was, without doubt, a lucky thing for his cycling reputation that he was defeated, as had he proved victorious he would probably have finally retired from the path, and the grand performances which he subsequently accomplished would not have been placed to his credit.

It was about this time that a course of action regarding highway by-laws was adopted, and this has since been steadily followed out by the NCU, to the great advantage of the cycling public. A memorial, opposing certain by-laws, was presented to the justices of the county of Cambridge, signed by upwards of seventy persons, of whom sixty were fellows or late fellows of colleges, including *inter alia* four fellows of the Royal Society, three professors of the University, eight past or present proctors, six deans of colleges, and several holders of the highest legal honours, chancellor's medallists, Whewell scholars, etc.

In the course of an article published about this date Mr Charles Spencer claims to have taught the late Charles Dickens to ride a bicycle, but he fell into an error, his pupil was Mr J. C. Parkinson, who wrote one or two papers on the subject at the time, and who, seated on the Brighton Coach, saw John Mayall, struggling along a few miles outside the Southern watering-place on the occasion of his succeeding in riding from London to Brighton in one day.

In February 1880 the season was duly opened according to precedent by the holding of the Stanley Show at the Holborn Town Hall, this locale replaced the Foresters' Hall by reason of its greater accommodation – soon, however, to be found in its turn too small. The show was an immense success, though the machines then exhibited would now be considered sadly heavy and old-fashioned.

In March the Surrey BC by resolution decided to accept no protest against any rider who had not broken the rules of the union. This action was taken in consequence of a threat on the part of some of the anti-union party to protest against Cortis because he had competed with Keen under union sanction.

On April 24 a most important athletic gathering was held at Oxford, whereat the Amateur Athletic Association was formed. The cyclists of the two Universities desired to be represented at this meeting, but the athletes decided not to admit them, having in view the fact that the cyclists already possessed a ruling body, and it was pretty generally understood among wheelmen at that time that cycling was to be left alone. Yet the only sport specifically mentioned in the first small leaflet circulated, containing a report of the proceedings, was cycling, a fact which raised a vast amount of feeling, which was only subdued when the Treaty of Fleet Street, as the arrangement now well known among cyclists was called, put things on a clear and indisputable footing between the NCU and the AAA.

Coventry at this time mounted its police officers upon the Silent Steed, and the fact was duly commented upon at some length in the *Daily News*, the writer facetiously suggesting that 'a defaulting debtor pursued by a constable mounted on a tricycle, and armed with a summons, sounds more like a horrible dream than a probable reality,' and quoted Tennyson: 'New men who, in the flying of a wheel, Cry down the past' as appropriate to the occasion.

The Hampton Court Meet was a great success, a large number being present, and distant towns – Tynemouth, Hull, Portsmouth, and others – were represented by a contingent of riders. Over 2,000 cyclists took part in the parade. In June Mr Frank W. Weston, an Englishman domiciled in the United

States, and the pioneer of American cycling, brought over a party of four Americans, the most prominent among them being Mr (now Judge) J. S. Dean of Boston. The visitors made a somewhat lengthy tour through the Midland and Southern districts, and were entertained at dinner in Coventry and London. A mysterious association, known to fame as the Connaught Rangers BC, held a race meeting late in August on the Surbiton track, and in the Ten Miles Scratch Race, H. L. Cortisrode in magnificent form, establishing a record for 10 miles inside 30 minutes, for the first time in cycling history, his time being 29 minutes, 54 seconds.

In August the North of England meet was held under the auspices of the Bradford BC at Harrogate, in Yorkshire, and led to the establishment of the Northern Cyclists' Camp, which under the energetic management of the same club has each year been a great success, a large number of wheelmen from all parts of the United Kingdom mustering under canvas for four days, at the beginning of August. In connection with this notable meet, a general meeting of the then Bicycle Touring Club took place in the concert-room of the Spa Grounds, Low Harrogate, at which an agenda of considerable length was submitted to the assembled members, some of whom had come long distances for the purpose of taking part in the deliberations. After a comparatively short session, it was suddenly announced that the room must be vacated for the evening concert, and the meeting was asked to adopt the rules submitted without consideration. A very heated discussion ensued, and was continued in a smaller room to which the meeting adjourned, a party dubbed the 'Malcontents' was formed, and they eventually secured the necessary reforms in the organisation of the club.

In riding southward from this meet, Mr Henry Sturmey, of *The Cyclist*, took particular note of the 26-inch handlebars which Mr Hillier had had fitted to his bicycle, and on 10 August his journal contained an able leader on the value of long handlebars. The fashion thus set withstood the test of time and experience, and has proved of value to young riders, a long handle-bar, as will be seen in the following chapters of this work, being particularly serviceable in assisting the novice to acquire a good style.

On September 2 Cortis made his first attempt to cover 20 miles in the hour, encouraged by his success at 10 miles above recorded. The Surbiton path was chosen and every effort was made to get it into good condition. This track was – in common with most London paths – then ridden right hand inside. A number of well-known cyclists were asked to assist as pacemakers. At 6.10 p.m. when the start took place, a very slight breeze was blowing which went down with the sun. The weather was warm, and singularly favourable. G. E. Liles tarted with Cortis and covered 2 miles in 6 minutes and 5 seconds when the record-breaker, not being satisfied with the rate of progression, went in front and covered the third mile in 2 minutes, 59 seconds. Liles made a dash at the end of 4 miles, when he gave way to J. F. Griffith, who with a flying start rode the next 4 miles in 11 minutes, 54 seconds, and thus knocked off the odd seconds for Cortis, whose time for 8 miles was 24 minutes, and three-fifths of a second. Sidney Kemp then came on, but he, like Liles, could not make pace, and at 12 miles Cortis was 245 seconds, outside even time. G. Lacy

Hillier took up the running, and forcing the pace for 2 miles he assisted the record-breaker to knock two seconds off his loss. Hillier then gave way to Griffith, who took Cortis along in excellent style, so that at 16 miles he was but eight seconds outside. Liles joining in, he and Griffith raced hard against one another, and the seventeenth mile was a very good one, being covered in 2 minutes, 52 seconds. Cortis being only one fifth of a second outside even time, Kemp joined the trio, and the eighteenth mile was completed in 52 minutes, 56 seconds or 3 seconds, inside evens. In the third lap of the nineteenth mile Liles, on the inside, swerved from exhaustion and came into collision with Griffith, the pair falling heavily right in front of Cortis, who came down over them, Kemp escaping in the most marvellous manner, just getting clear of Cortis' machine. Cortis was not very much hurt beyond flesh wounds, but J. F. Griffith broke his ankle, and the shock of the fall severely injured his heart, although this was not discovered till much later. The mile times from eleven to eighteen were then best on record. The *Daily Telegraph* based a lengthy and amusing article upon Cortis' feat, in which, among other remarks emphasising the value of the new sport, the writer said,

> Not the worst thing that they have done, these knights of the road, has been to rehabilitate and set on their legs again many of our old posting-houses and decayed hostelries all over the country. Bicycles have to a certain extent taken the place of coaches, they frequent all our great main roads, and gladden the hearts of innkeepers, who look out for the tinkling bells which herald the advent of a "club" of

wandering velocipedists, just as they anticipated of yore the gladsome tootling of the horn that bespoke the approach of the Enterprize, the Highflyer, or some other well-known conveyance of the old coaching days.

A fortnight later Cortis made another attempt to ride 20 miles in the hour, but he had in the interval had another fall while racing at Lincoln, and was decidedly unfit, under these circumstances he failed to approach his former times, falling very weak in the fourteenth mile, and being 38 seconds, outside the hour when 20 miles had been covered. The rider was awfully disgusted when Coleman told him that he was outside the limit, but doubling testily to his work he dashed on for 5 miles more, covering 25 miles in 1 hour, 16 minutes; 41 seconds, which stood as a best on record until 1886, when the time was beaten on a modern path by J. E. Fenlon. Cortis won the Surrey Cup for the third time at the autumn meeting, and thus became its absolute possessor.

On October 9 the once celebrated Crystal Palace track was opened by a grand-race meeting, the programme included a challenge cup for a club team race, and a one mile handicap. The day was a dreadful one, and the new track very heavy in consequence. G. Lacy Hillier won both events from scratch in very slow time. On 6 November the second Fifty Miles Road Tricycle Championship was promoted by the Finchley and London TCs jointly, the course being from Tally Ho Corner. Finchley, N., to a point just this side of Hitchin and back. Fifteen men in all started. The morning was very foggy, and the trains were late. Consequently Hillier, who had been training for the event, and who practically introduced the double-steering Humber tricycle to London riders in this contest, eventually started 13 minutes after the other competitors, but at 12 miles from the start he had passed everyone except Vesey, who was only one minute in front of him at this point. Vesey was riding a 'bicycle' fitted with two small hind wheels, which public opinion universally decided was an unfair machine, and eventually won somewhat easily, Hillier finishing second, C. Crute third, R. C. Baker fourth, G. D. Godbolt fifth, and H. L. Cortis sixth. The Tricycle Association, then recently formed, established a remarkable and utterly impracticable 'amateur definition' but this body – minus its definition – was eventually absorbed into the Bicycle, or as it is now termed the National Cyclists Union.

Yet another great advance is that recorded for 1880. *The Cyclist*, started in the last month of 1879, came very strongly to the front, and, supporting the governing body of cycling in contradistinction to the attitude assumed by some of the other papers, took a leading place in that section of journalism.

In February 1881 the season was opened in the orthodox manner by the holding of the fifth Stanley Show – for the second time at the Holborn Town Hall. A steam tricycle, the invention of Sir Thomas Parkyns, was shown on this occasion, but the requirements of the law as regards steam-driven vehicles G 2-put a complete check upon the development of the invention, of which nothing has since been heard.

News from Cairo about this time recorded the fact that a Mr E. F. Rogers had ridden from that city to the pyramid of Cheops, thus bringing two vastly distant cycles into close approximation, while within a week or two it was announced that Prince Yeo, son of the King of Siam, Lord of the Thousand White Elephants, etc., had purchased a bicycle for his own use.

The union accepted the principle of movable championships for the first time, and ran two of its four contests in the Midlands. The principle then adopted has proved of inestimable value to the ruling body of cycling, as it has brought the leading men of the various sections and districts into actual contact, and extended and developed in a most valuable manner the resources of the union. Much of the accord which now exists between the various centres and the Executive is due entirely to the intercourse in connection with the promotion of the championship contests.

On May 21, 2,050 riders attended the Hampton Court meet, and the weather being fine the sight was an exceedingly picturesque one, while later on 136 tricyclists met on Ealing Common and paraded with great effect, the tricycle lending itself much more easily to that sort of work than the unstable bicycle.

On June 25 the third Fifty Miles Road Race for the tricycle championship was run under singularly unpleasant conditions, and over muddy and stony roads, from Hounslow via Maidenhead and Cookham to a point 25 miles out and back. The race fell to G. Lacy Hillier in 4 hours, 53 minutes. On July 6 the NCU held at Surbiton its first championship for the Five Miles, which fell to G. Lacy Hillier by 80 yards, after a good race with Liles, Palmer, and Milner, this being the first occasion on which a really representative Midlander had visited London to compete for championship honours.

C. A. Palmer, waited on by Liles, stuck closely to Hillier's hind wheel during the first 4 miles, Milner making all the running. 21 laps from home Hillier dashed to the front, and sustaining his spurt, Palmer cracked just after the bell, and Hillier drew away and won easily in 15 minutes, 39 seconds.

On the 16th Hillier won the One and Twenty-five Miles Championships at Belgrave Road Grounds, Leicester, the final of the Mile being a match between Hillier and Liles. A very slow pace was set by the former till the bell rang, when he sprang off at top speed and won by six yards, making a best on record for a flying quarter mile, 36 seconds. In the Twenty-Five Miles he also won easily by 40 yards, C. Crute second, C. E. Liles third. On 21 July Hillier established a mile grass record, covering that distance, at Priory Park, Chichester, in 2 minutes, 51 seconds. On 27 July Hillier won the last championship of the year, by 30 yards from C. Crute, J. F. Griffith third, 2 hours, 50 minutes; 50 seconds, best on record by nearly 4 minutes. He thus won the five open championships of 1881.

The first Northern Cyclists' Camp was held at Harrogate in August. Although rain fell heavily most of the time, the campers so far managed to enjoy themselves that the camp has become one of the best and most enjoyable holidays a cyclist has to look forward to.

On 3 June 1882, H. L. Cortis, who had been doing a good deal of riding, competed at the Crystal Palace in the West Kent BC's Open Mile Handicap, of course from scratch, and in the sixth heat beat the mile record, covering that distance in 2 minutes, 43 seconds, the last lap being a marvelous one. The previous records were: amateur, Keith-Falconer's 2 minutes,

46 seconds; professional, Fred Cooper's 2 minutes, 46 seconds, while on the 7th Cortis again reduced the time on the Surbiton path in the One Mile Invitation Handicap of the Wanderers BC, covering the mile in 2 minutes, 41 seconds. On the same evening Cortis had a try at Keith-Falconer's 2-mile time, but failed to beat it by 2 seconds. The Hon. Ion Keith-Falconer, who is practically the father of Land's End to John O' Groat's rides, went over the celebrated route in 12 days, 23 hours, 15 minutes, a very grand performance at the time, though it looks very small alongside later developments. About this time an Oxford man, H. R. Reynolds, went over the 'Turpin route', from London to York, a distance of 196 miles, in 21 hours, 43 minutes. His predecessor was W. T. Thorn of the L.BC, whose machine broke down some few miles out of York as previously related.

The first union championships ever held in Birmingham came off on July 8, when Frank Moore won both the One Mile and the Twenty-five Miles. On the 9th W. F. Sutton, of the London Scottish, on an ordinary bicycle covered 222 miles on the Great North Road in 23 hours, 55 minutes, riding time 21 hours, which it is needless to say was the best on record. On 22 July, J. S. Whatton, the flying Cantab, won the Five Miles Amateur Championship on the Crystal Palace in 15 minutes, 121 seconds, Keith-Falconer being second, and C. Crute third, while on the 29th Keith-Falconer handsomely won the Fifty Miles Amateur Championship from C. D. Vesey and W. K. Adams in 2 hours, 43 minutes, 58 seconds, a best on record by nearly 7 minutes. Vesey broke a spoke 2 miles from the finish. This was indeed a busy week at the Crystal Palace track, as W. K. Adams covered 3 miles in 8 minutes, 4 seconds, a best on record, and H. L. Cortis at last accomplished the feat he had so often attempted, and covered 20 miles in the hour. It was a model evening, with not a breath of wind. The flags hung motionless against the posts. Cortis was assisted by Woolnough, Hunter, Vesey, Tacagni, Adams, and last but by no means least Alfred Thompson. Well coached, led and clocked, Cortis covered the 20 miles in 50 minutes, 31 seconds, and 20 miles 300 yards in the hour. He rode a 60-inch Invincible. Not satisfied with this grand performance, Cortis desired to make yet another attempt, and at last, to the delight of all sportsmen, it was announced that Cortis and Keith-Falconer would ride 20 miles together. There had long been a desire to see these two great riders meet, and a crowd visited Surbiton on August 2. Pacemakers, including Messers Adams, Woolnough, Tacagni, McKinlay and others. Up to 6 miles Falconer retained the post he had taken up, dead on Cords' hind wheel. But he was palpably labouring, though the fact was not within Cortis' ken. Peter McKinlay taking the post of pacemaker at this juncture, set a hot pace, and in the second lap, along the top of the ground, Falconer was beaten, Cortis looking under his arm, took in the situation at a glance, and shouting excitedly 'Go on, Peter,' he doubled to his work in a moment, and left the Cantab, who shortly afterwards gave up. From 7 miles every record was beaten up to 20 miles in 59 minutes, 20 seconds, and 20 miles 325 yards were covered in an hour.

This year Harrogate Camp was favoured with fine weather and was a pronounced success in every way. In the latter part of the month the Wanderers gave a farewell dinner to H. L. Cortis, who shortly afterwards departed with his newly married wife to Australia. It was with the deepest regret that the wheel world heard of his early death at Carcoar, New South Wales, on 28 December 1885, of a complication resulting from low fever caused by the climate. After his arrival in the colonies Cortis did little or no cycling, but rode several horses in steeplechases, in the course of which the ex-champion broke his arm, though he had never broken a bone from his bicycle. He named one of his steeplechasers 'Lacy Hillier' because it could stay, in kindly remembrance of an old friend. The private and personal friends of Cortis have erected in the church of Ripley, in Surrey – a spot much frequented by cyclists – a window and brass to his memory, which will long be honoured wherever cyclists most do congregate.

On 14 October the union promoted its first Tricycle championship, distance 5 miles. There was an excellent entry, and after a fine struggle the race fell to C. E. Liles, H. W. Gaskell second, the much fancied Midlander, M. J. Lowndes, was disposed of by the winner in the second round.

In November the members of the Tricyclist Conference met at supper to signalise the success of the road race they had promoted, and the establishment of a 'new T.A.' was first mooted. This was soon attempted, but a majority of practical tricyclists were opposed to the movement, and The Tricycle Union at last ceased to exist shortly after an unsuccessful attempt to promote an 'Amateur Championship' at the Crystal Palace track.

On December 14, at a council meeting of the union, certain

suspended riders appealed to the council for reinstatement. Mr W. B. Tanner took the lead on behalf of the executive, Mr T. E. Scrutton occupying the chair. The appellants requiring some assistance, the chairman asked if any gentleman – preferably a legal man – among the delegates present would undertake to assist them. Then, in the words of an amusing skit written at the time: 'Someone with legal bent, deep voice, and twinkling eyes, rises to the occasion.' This was Mr Robert Todd, of the Stanley BC, a newly elected councillor, who soon after became honorary secretary to the union, to its immense advantage, and so this year closed with much promise for the future.

The Stanley Show, held at the Albert Hall in January, was the first notable event of 1883, but the big rambling building, with its many square yards of unavailable space, its tortuous passages and poor light, was by no means suitable for the purposes of the show, which nevertheless attracted a numerous crowd of visitors, including a strong contingent of West End people, whom the associations of the hall, and curiosity, brought to view the exhibits.

It is recorded that a cyclist in the spring of this year rode his bicycle for half an hour on the Goodwin Sands. Why he went there is a mystery, but the fact remains: a bicycle has been ridden on the Goodwins.

The Hampton Court meet was duly held, though scarcely so well supported as before, an increasing number of leading clubs standing out. Eastern and Western civilisation was brought into pretty close contact, as a Japanese jinricksha was taken alongside the procession for some distance.

Early in this year the Bicycle Touring Club, after lengthy

consideration, changed its name to that under which it now exists: the Cyclists' Touring Club, or CTC, these letters replacing the then more favoured formula BTC.

About this time C. H. R. Gosset covered just over 200 miles in the 24 hours on a tricycle, the first time this feat was accomplished on the road.

Early in July, Alfred Thompson of the Sutton BC cut two of Cortis' records at the Brixton Ramblers' meeting at the Crystal Palace, covering the starting quarter in 40 seconds, and the half mile in 1 min, 19 seconds. The Hon. Ion Keith-Falconer's Land's End to John O' Groat's record was beaten by James Lennox of Dumfries, who rode the distance in 9 days, 4 hours, 40 minutes, thus beating the previous record by nearly four days.

On July 7 two of the union Championships were held at Aston Lower Grounds, Birmingham. The Five Miles Bicycle Championship fell to F. Sutton. C. E. Liles easily secured the One Mile Tricycle Championship from M. J. Lowndes in 3 minutes, 18 seconds.

In July the London T.C. organised a great 24 hours race on tricycles, the course being from Caterham Junction near Croydon to Brighton, thence along the coast to Fareham, thence via Romsey and Salisbury and on through Stockbridge and Alton, as far as the riders could go in the 24 hours, no less than 74 entries were obtained, of whom 67 started at midnight on Friday 6 July, and it was truly a marvellous sight that met the eye, as 67 tricycles bearing one or more lamps, together with a great crowd of cyclists who were present as spectators, moved off along the dark glade of Smitham's Bottom. Ripley, distant some 202 miles from the start, was regarded as likely to prove the destination, especially when the breeze freshened as the day broke, and several men arranged to ride down on Saturday to see the finish. Those who went down early, however, were startled about 8.45 p.m. in the evening by the receipt of a wire from Mr T. Griffith, who was checking at Alton, announcing that Marriott had passed there at 7.01 p.m. At 9.30 p.m. John Keen, on a bicycle, dashed into Ripley and ordered tea, and at 9.39 p.m. T. R. Marriott, the first man, rode up, going strongly and well. After a mouthful of tea, he pushed on, and riding out the time, reached Merton, 218.75 miles, at 11.50 p.m. Nixon was the second man to reach Ripley, which he did at 10.23 p.m., and having no friend to keep him going, he went to bed, and while he slept Vesey, who arrived at 10.29 p.m., pushed painfully on to Wisley Common and back, and took second place with a score of 205.25 miles, the last 5.25 miles taking him 1 hour, 15 minutes to cover. Gosset, arriving at 11.41 p.m., rode a quarter of a mile farther up the road and back, and thus took third place.

Marriott's time was a best on record, while all the four men beat Gosset's record of 200 miles in 24 hours. In July, the then Lord Bury, whose efforts to bring about an amicable arrangement between the B. U. and the T. U. had been frustrated by the executive of the latter body, who repudiated the arrangement they had empowered him to propose, resigned the Presidency of the Tricycle Union, and was subsequently unanimously elected President of the B. U. (now NCU), his acceptance of office marking a new era of increased prosperity and success for the Jockey Club of the sport.

On the 14th, the One Mile Bicycle and Ten Miles Tricycle Championships were competed for on the Crystal Palace track, the mile falling to H. W. Gaskell, who was followed home by Alfred Thompson – F. Sutton, who was much fancied, falling in the second lap, time 2 minutes, 55 seconds. The Tricycle Championship fell to C. E. Liles in 33 minutes, 45 seconds, M. J. Lowndes being second.

The Crichton BC's evening meeting on the following Thursday was notable for the fact that the 4 miles record was twice beaten. H. F. Wilson covered the distance in the fifth heat in 11 minutes, 37 seconds, while in the final H. W. Gaskell won in 11 minutes, 34 seconds, Wilson declining to start. Wilson won the Fifty Miles Championship on the 21st in 2 hours, 46 minutes, 26 seconds, from F. R. Fry of Clifton.

On the 27th F. R. Fry of Clifton beat all bicycle records from 51 miles to 100 on the Crystal Palace track, covering the full distance in 5 hours, 50 minutes, 5 seconds, which still remains, at time of writing, a best on record.

The Twenty-five Miles Bicycle Championship fell to C. E. Liles in 1 hour, 22 minutes, 42 seconds, the race being run at Taunton on 2 August. On the same day James Lennox beat the existing 24 hours bicycle road record by covering 229 miles in the specified time.

The Harrogate meet was once more a pronounced success, being favoured with excellent weather, and everything passing off in the most satisfactory style. Lennox's record was not long permitted to stand, as Mr J. W. M. Brown on 16 August covered 255.25 miles on the road in 24 hours, a grand performance.

On September 8, the Tricycle Conference promoted what proved to be the last Fifty Miles Road Championship Race. For some considerable time the more far-seeing members of the cycling body had recognised the fact that the practice of holding open races on the road was illegal and likely to prove detrimental to the credit and interests of the cycling sport, and as a consequence much opposition was manifested. The Tricycle Conference, however, rather braved the matter out, inserting advertisements, not only in the cycling, but in the sporting press. A few hours before the race the managers were notified that the police were on the qui vive on the chosen route, so at the 11th hour the course was changed, the start taking place at Caterham Junction, and the line running through Oxted, Westerham, and River Head to Ightham and back. The men were despatched at minute intervals, and no police interference took place at the start, nineteen men in all being sent off. A number of riders went out to meet the returning competitors, some of whom awaited them at the top of the hill out of Godstone, and here Marriott was sighted – hatless and smothered in dust. Mat Sinclair, the Scottish champion, set a fair pace for him on a tricycle, while Messers G. L. Hillier and C. E. Liles rode quietly along some few yards in the rear. When within a mile of home an approaching pony carriage was suddenly drawn across the road, and a constable in blue and another in plain clothes stopped the leader and the accompanying trio and took their names and addresses, Marriott going off at top speed the moment he was released, to the intense disgust of the officers, who hastily jumping into the trap made an unavailing effort to catch him. Marriott won by 25 minutes from George Smith, W. Bourdon being third. No further action was taken by the police except the issue of the following notice:

Persons using bicycles, including tricycles, are hereby cautioned that such vehicles are carriages within the meaning of the Highway and Metropolitan Police Acts. Furious driving (Taylor vs. Goodwin decided by the judges, 25 March 1879). The Metropolitan Police Acts impose a penalty on any person who shall ride or drive furiously, or so as to endanger the life or limb of any person, or to the common danger of the passengers in any thoroughfare. The police are directed to ascertain the names and addresses of persons about to take part in any bicycle or tricycle race within the metropolitan police district, or to proceed against, and, if necessary, to take into custody, any persons violating the above law. The provisions of the law as to obstructions are independent of the above.

It will be easily seen that the road race, being obviously an illegal contest, even if it had done no more than necessitate the issuing such a notice, had already accomplished more harm than good to the sport of cycling.

C. E. Liles won the Surrey Cup at the autumn meeting in 34 minutes. 69 seconds.

The Times contained in October a letter signed D. C. L., in which the writer stated that although he had suffered for twenty-five years from a spinal affection which rendered it impossible for him to undergo a journey by train or vehicle, he 'had just undertaken a bicycle tour through Sussex of 115 miles'. He added that, throughout the trip, he had not only felt better in health, but had absolutely been in less physical pain than at any other period during the previous quarter of a century. Without doubt the affection in this case must have been partly nervous, the novelty and excitement of the exercise taking the sufferer's attention somewhat from his troubles.

W. F. Sutton made an attempt upon the 24 hours bicycle road record with success, covering 260.25 miles in that time, while a few days later J. S. Smith and his wife on an Invincible sociable rode 10 miles on the Palace track in 41 minutes, 40 seconds, best on record.

1884, destined to be an important cycling year, opened with a meeting of lady members of the CTC, who discussed in camera the details of a suitable costume, and in the end a decision was come to mainly upon the practical experiences of Mrs J. S. Smith, Miss Choice, and several other well-known lady riders, the result being in every way satisfactory.

In March the Birmingham Local Centre of the NCU initiated the very valuable agitation for improved roads, which has been so energetically followed up. A great meeting was held under the presidency of the Mayor of Birmingham, at which cyclists, horse-owners, and horse-users banded themselves together to promote the agitation, and subsequently action was taken against sundry road surveyors with satisfactory results. As a consequence the union has now some very convincing precedents to lay before road surveyors who object to a demand on the part of cyclists for improved highways.

The Hampton Court meet was finally abandoned in this year, the general view being that 'monster meets' had served their purpose and were not likely to do the sport further service. At the end of May a Cyclists' Camp was held at the Alexandra Palace on the same lines as the Harrogate Camp, but proved a complete failure. The one redeeming point was some excellent racing.

On June 21 the first two of the Championship contests were held at Lillie Bridge (new track), the mile falling to H. A. Speechley, after a waiting race, C. E. Liles being second, and H. W. Gaskell third, time: 3 minutes, 30 seconds. The Twenty-five Miles Tricycle was won by C. E. Liles, H. J. Webb second, Sidney Lee third; 1 hour, 28 minutes, 58 seconds, best on record.

Chambers walked over for the Five Miles Championship at Cardiff, time 15 minutes, 36 seconds, on 28 June. On the same day the official timekeeper at the West Kent BC meeting returned, Alfred Thompson's mile time in the fourth heat of the open mile was 2 minutes, 39 seconds, giving the quarter mile times, which he had been specially requested by Mr G. Pembroke Coleman (who was away at the Championship) to note, as Thompson's private form pointed to his doing something good. A dead set was, however, made at the record, and it was not put upon the book. Thompson held at this time the half-mile record, and had only a week or two before been deprived of the starting quarter record. He ran a trial during the following week, but was very nervous, and a pacemaker falling at the start upset him altogether, and he did nothing. The same evening G. L. Hillier made record for a flying quarter: time, 35 seconds, thus beating J. S. Whatton's 36 seconds.

The Ten Miles Championship of the North, run on the Wallsend track on 12 July, fell to R. H. English in 30 minutes, 14 seconds, and caused that sterling rider to take a foremost place in the opinion of amateur cycledom. On the same date the Five and Twenty-five Miles Tricycle Championships were run off on the Crystal Palace track, C. E. Liles winning both, H. J. Webb finishing second in the mile: time, 3 minutes, 29 seconds, and Sidney Lee in the 5 mile: time, 18 minutes, 8 seconds.

On 14 July the Fifty Miles Amateur Championship fell to F. R. Fry of Clifton, after a splendid race with C. S. Wadey, F. J. Nicolas third: time, 2 hours, 51 minutes, 16 seconds.

On July 26 the holding of the Twenty-five Miles Amateur Championship brought to the front R. H. English of North Shields. The race was run on the North Durham track, a small and by no means fast path, Speechley, Robinson, and Nicolas representing London, they waited at the start, but English was off like a shot out of a gun, and fairly left the lot, lapping all his opponents and winning anyhow in 1 hour, 22 minutes, 4/5 second, on a wet and heavy track, D. H. Huie was second, and J. Tough third.

M. Josef Kohout, of the Cesky Velociped Klub, Prague – a splendid specimen of the Continental cyclist – rode 220.5 English miles, from Hamburg via Kiel to Flensburg, and back to Bonningstedt, in 24 hours, and as he had to lift his heavy old-fashioned roadster over innumerable gates in the dark, this performance becomes the more remarkable.

On 11 September R. H. English made his debut on a London

path in the Crystal Palace Challenge Cup race, distance: 15 miles. A fairly good field opposed him, but he dashed off the mark at a tremendous pace, and covered the first mile in 2 minutes, 42 seconds, or only a fraction outside record, 20 yards short of the mile William Brown, who had hung on to him up to this point, cracked, and English went right away, and beat every record from 2 to 20 miles – keeping on after winning the race for the purpose of securing the records.

In the five miles race for the Kildare Cup, run at Lillie Bridge on the following Saturday, English pursued the same tactics, and though not riding nearly so fast, the first mile taking 2 minutes, 48 seconds, he left Speechley in the first quarter of the second mile, and won again anyhow. The big Tynesider never did better than on this occasion, some severe falls, and a desire to spurt fast for short distances, decidedly did him no good subsequently.

On September 27 a curious contest was decided between Major T. Knox Holmes, a veteran tricyclist of seventy-eight, and Mr G. Lacy Hillier, a bicyclist of twenty-eight, the latter conceding the former a start of one mile for every year's difference in their respective ages in a 10 hour race. The veteran only dismounted for a trifle over 5 minutes, while the bicyclist stopped for over 35 minutes. The scores at the finish were: Major Knox Holmes: 115 miles, 101 to 115 being records, and G. L. Hillier: 146 miles, 51 to 54 and 101 to 146 being records. The Major thus won easily. The day was very unfavourable, being windy and wet.

1884 closed in a somewhat perturbed manner. Several road performances were being openly questioned in the public press, and the union was engaged in investigating the bona fides of the various claims. An agitation was also in progress concerning the way round for racing paths, which ultimately resulted in the almost universal adoption of the left-hand inside practice of riding. The annual meeting of the CTC was held in London, and certain revolutionary doctrines with regard to the internal management of the club, which had been discussed in a blustering and ferocious manner in the papers, were advocated at the meeting in mild and mellifluous terms, singularly in contrast with the earlier steps of the dispute, the voting, however, showed a large majority in favour of the status quo ante.

In 1885 commenced the great struggle between the NCU and the A. A. A., the dispute being originated by some of the most prominent of the supporters of the dissolved Liverpool Local Centre. After a struggle the union obtained all the points for which it had felt obliged in the interests of cycling to contend, thus becoming without any question the sole ruling body of cycling.

S. Sellers won the One Mile Championship at Lower Aston Grounds, Birmingham, by 6 inches from W. A. Illston, on 13 June, time: 2 minutes, 47 seconds, and R. Cripps the Five Miles Tricycle Championship in 16 minutes, 53 seconds. G. Gatehouse being second.

Webber won the Five Miles Amateur Championship on 27 June, at Jarrow track, in 14 minutes, 22 seconds, after one of the finest races ever seen in a championship contest, D. W. Laing being second, and R. Chambers third. July produced another crop of records. On 6 July Mrs Allen of Birmingham covered 200 miles on the road in 23 hours. 54 minutes, and

C. H. R. Gosset covered 231.75 miles inside 24 hours.

On 11 July the NCU held its One and Twenty-five Miles Tricycle Championships on the Crystal Palace track, and the contests proved most exciting. P. Furnivall won the One Mile Championship alter a dead heat with P. T. Letch ford in 3 minutes, 5 seconds, having, made a best on record in his heat : time, 2 minutes. 585 seconds. The Twenty-five Miles Championship was won in splendid style by George Gatehouse, who made most of the running, records were made for 2 and 3 miles, and from 11 to 2 miles. He covered the full distance in 1 hour, 26 minutes, 29 seconds.

On July 9 Webber beat the mile record on the Crystal Palace track, doing 2 minutes, 39 seconds. On 18 July R. H. English won the Fifty Miles Championship from G. Gatehouse in 2 hours, 45 minutes, 13 seconds, record being beaten by English, Gatehouse, and Nicolas from 29 to 38 miles inclusive. English also won the Twenty-five Miles Championship at the Ayleston Road Grounds, Leicester, time 1 hour, 20 minutes, 13 seconds, R. Cripps second, and W. Terry third. The Harrogate Camp was again a marked success, while a southern camp at Tunbridge Wells was also successful.

G. Lacy Hillier visited Leipsic in September, and defeated Johann Pundt, the amateur champion of Germany and others in a 10,000 metres scratch race, beating the German record at the same time, and bringing back one of the finest prizes ever given for a cycle race.

In November the CTC accepted with much regret the resignation of its Chairman, Mr N. F. Duncan, who had done good service to the club during his period of office. Mr Duncan resigned as he was just about to take holy orders in the Church of England.

On 16 January, 1886, the A. A. A. meeting at Anderton's Hotel, Fleet Street, passed a resolution by which 'the war', as it was termed, which had created no end of trouble and annoyance, was put an end to. Since this time the two associations have worked hand in hand for the benefit of amateur sport.

In February the cycling world was startled by the receipt of the sad news that Herbert Liddell Cortis, the ex-amateur champion at all distances in 1879 and three distances in 1880, was dead. One of the most popular of men, and in the opinion of many good judges the best rider that ever crossed a wheel, the memory of H. L. Cortis will always remain green in the annals of cycling.

H. A. Speechley won the Surrey Cup for the third time, thus making it his property, as Cortis had done before him, P. Furnivall finishing second, and A. E. Langley third: time, 41 minutes, 44 seconds.

The tricyclists forgathered at Hampton Court in May, the meet including nearly 500 riders of the broad-gauge machine, and proving highly successful. At the Gainsborough meeting H. A. Speechley cut his own starting quarter record, doing 38 seconds.

The first of the championship meetings was held at Weston-super-Mare on the new track on 14 July, 1886. The One Mile Tricycle Championship fell to Percy Furnivall: time, 3 minutes, 5 seconds. The Twenty-five Miles Bicycle Championship fell to J. E. Fenlon: time, 1 hour 19 minutes, 29 seconds, the fastest Twenty-five Miles Championship ever ridden up to that time.

On 19 June the North Road Club promoted a 50 miles race open to all sorts of cycles, some mischievous persons sent letters to the police authorities signed with the name of a cyclist who was known to object to these races, but no trouble ensued. The ordinary bicycles were set to concede the tandems a start, but were not in the hunt. The race was handsomely won by C. E. Liles and A. J. Wilson: time, 3 hours, 16 minutes, 58 seconds, J. Lee and G. Gatehouse second: time, 3 hours, 23 minutes, 16 seconds.

The One Mile Championship was run on 26 June on the Jarrow track, and proved in every way a success, victory resting with Percy Furnivall, H. A. Speechley second, and W. A. Illston third: time, 2 minutes, 46 seconds, one of the finest races ever seen for what is practically the blue ribbon of cycling.

F. W. Allard made a record for the tricycle mile at Long Eaton on the same day: time, 2 minutes, 54 seconds, while F. J. Osmond and S. E. Williams, at the Crystal Palace, covered 2 miles in 5 minutes, 47 seconds, a record for the distance.

One of the most astonishing feats of the year was performed by George P. Mills, of the Anfield BC, who, leaving Land's End at midnight on 4 July, reached John O' Groat's in 5 days, 1 hour, 45 minutes. The distance is 861 miles, and he only slept for six hours in all during the journey. At the end of 1886 it may be safely asserted that the sport of cycling was fully established in popular estimation, and its progress has been quite as rapid since that date as it was before.

The more recent history of cycling is a matter of common knowledge. Papers, daily and weekly, have given an increasing amount of space to the racing and other branches of the sport, and the developments have been steady in all directions. The Jubilee year was made the occasion of a very singular demonstration. The cyclists of the United Kingdom, acting on the suggestion of Mr Henry Sturmey, of Coventry, subscribed over £800 to present a lifeboat called *The Cyclist* to the port of West Hartlepool, where the boat was formally launched at a public ceremony on 17 December 1887. Since then the lifeboat has done good service, and the cyclists of the United Kingdom have paid the expenses, amounting to some £70 a year. Over 6,000 individual subscribers supported the fund. The movement was discussed in the press, and the public spirit of the rapidly increasing army of wheelmen was commended in many quarters.

Military cycling has advanced most rapidly in recent years, and has unquestionably established itself in public estimation as a useful branch of the volunteer service. Those enthusiasts who went to work, not wisely but too well, in the earlier days have 'burnt out' and the less imaginative but more practical men have come to the front. The movement has grown out of leading strings, and bids fair to take a reasonable place in the service. Perhaps the most singular and significant of its developments is the existence of what is really a body of volunteer military cyclists within the ranks of the regular army. This remarkable corps has been formed by Major Edye, of the Royal Marine Light Infantry, at Walmer, assisted by Lieutenants Anderson and Connolly, and it has proved very successful, despite the fact that the authorities, beyond giving permission to Major Edye to make the experiment, have done nothing towards helping the corps to purchase machines or outfits, and as the men have to devote what would otherwise be their leisure to attaining perfection in cycle drill, it can safely be said that any services which may in future be rendered by the cycle-mounted soldier will have been made possible to a very great extent by the labours of Major Edye and those who have worked with him.

It is singular, at first sight, to read of a Marine Cycle Corps. The 'Horse Marines' beloved of the fabulist, could hardly seem more incongruous, but as a matter of fact the cycle should prove a really serviceable 'horse' for the use of marines, in as much as many cycles could be stowed aboard ship, and would need neither care nor food till wanted for active service. Colonel Savile, Major Balfour, and others devoted themselves to the subject, and there can be no question but that it will continue to spread, and that the sport on the one hand and the volunteer movement on the other will be mutually benefited.

The more active branches of the sport have continued to grow apace. Touring, watched over by the Cyclists' Touring Club, has spread farther afield, and when Messrs G. W. Burston and H. R. Stokes, the Australian round-the-world tourists, arrived in England, they were loud in praise of the gigantic organisation which had smoothed their path. Periodical attacks upon the secretary and editor are made, but Mr Shipton has so often shown that he labours heart and soul for the big club, that there is always a solid majority of sturdy and undemonstrative members to back him when need arises. The cycling tourist is now to be encountered all over the continent, and the Cyclists' Touring Club has done a great work in educating the public, and especially the hotel and inn keepers, up to the proper appreciation of the army of touring wheel men and women, an army daily recruited from all classes of society.

The National Cyclists' Union continues to do good work in a quiet fashion, and, considering the meagre support accorded it by the cycling world from a financial point of view, it is astonishing how much it has affected. The discipline of the sport has been carefully maintained, the annual series of amateur championships contested, and the interests of cyclists carefully watched.

It is worthy of note that the universal by-laws for the regulation of cycle traffic, so long an important feature in the union's programme, have at last become an accomplished fact, after years of labour. At one time every local authority exercised its own sweet will in the matter of cycling by-laws.

A bell was required in one place, a whistle in another, lamps lit at sunset or earlier, and many other absurd regulations were enforced. All this has now been changed, and the hour of lamp-lighting – one hour after sunset – is the same all over the country, while the wheelman is also required to give audible warning of his approach.

On the racing path advances of a most significant kind have been made. The records of the giants of the past sink into insignificance as compared with those of the riders of today. New tracks of vastly improved construction are laid or being projected, and the whole section has made a step forward.

The advances made in the racing department, the innumerable records made today, to be beaten tomorrow, the difficulties of the handicappers, and the step by step development of the various types of machine upon the racing path, the best trial ground – the trial ground whereon almost every important cycling advance has been primarily tested and eventually developed – would take too long to detail at length in this chapter. The final result can best be gauged by the 'common measure' of time, though even this test fails to convey in all cases the exact results arrived at, in as much as training to sprint without training to stay may for the time being, at any rate, give to certain figures a fictitious importance. In this connection the tricycle records credited to Mr E. B. Turner may be instanced. Mr Turner is a gentleman who made a name for himself as an amateur runner some years ago. At a time when many men give up athletics he took to tricycling, and he has reduced the art of training and riding with pacemakers to a science. In 1890 he accomplished, upon a solid-tired tricycle, times which, in some cases, were then world's records for any sort of cycle!

On the whole the racing side of cycling shows a great advance. Promoting bodies should bear in mind that the finer shades of cycle-racing tactics only appeal to the cognoscenti, and that what the public like is a short sharp race, with a close finish, or a contest of champions from scratch.

An historical occasion, and one which cannot be passed over in silence in connection with anything purporting to be a history of cycling, must not be left unrecorded. It was arranged that on 5 July 1890, HRH the Prince of Wales visited Paddington Recreation Ground, and for the first time on record witness a series of cycle races. The arrangements were placed in the hands of the late Lord Randolph Churchill, Mr Melville Beachcroft, L. C. C., and Mr E. B. Turner, and the latter gentleman practically took the whole of the cycling work upon his shoulders, and made the three 'royal handicaps,' which were really masterpieces in their way. Unfortunately the chosen day turned out wet, and, somewhat unwisely, the meeting was postponed till the succeeding 9 Wednesday July when the weather was scarcely any better. The track was wet, but happily not flooded, and the arrangements were very complete indeed. Punctually to time the royal party drove into the enclosure, their Royal Highnesses being driven to a dais placed inside the running track, opposite the finish, and as soon as the address had been read by Lord Randolph Churchill and the Prince had made a suitable reply, the sport began. The One Mile Tricycle

Handicap fell to Lewis Stroud, Oxford U. B. C., 10 yards, start, A. H. Tubbs, 30 yards, 2nd, B. W. Crump, 20 yards, 3rd, H. H. Sansom.

Every man did his best to secure the result aimed at when the handicap was made, the establishment of a record. Of the scratch pair, Synyer most loyally assisted His co-marksman, riding the first quarter in 37 seconds. Osmond then dashed away, reaching the half-mile in 1 minute, 13 seconds, a record, and three-quarters in 1 minute, 55 seconds. Here the whole field were bunched, and rounding the bottom corner Osmond found his way through, and, riding with tremendous determination, won by 6 feet in 2 minutes, 3 seconds, tying his own record. The handicap was made to beat 2 minutes, 3 seconds. If it weren't for the wet, which made the track rather holding, Osmond would doubtless have created new figures.

At the conclusion of the 'royal handicaps,' HRH the Princess of Wales graciously intimated that she would present the prizes to the fortunate winners, which she did, and the royal party shortly afterwards left the ground amid loud cheers from the assembled crowds.

In this chapter the history of the cycling sport has been traced from the days of the Hobby Horse and the Draisnene, to the time when it has become an established and recognised form of sport adopted by young and old of both sexes. Much of the earlier history of the sport was forgotten when the first edition of this volume saw the light, and many a writer has availed himself of the information therein contained. In the future developments will, it is to be hoped, continue, but they will be more developments in detail. The sport is full grown, and waxes daily in public favour, recruits of both sexes are flocking to the ranks of cycling, and the practical everyday use of the wheel as a means of locomotion is becoming more and more general. The sportsman, the cricketer, the rowing man, the tennis player, reaches his destination upon the cycle, the tourist finds in it the acme of suitability as a touring vehicle, the tradesman adopts it vicariously for despatching his wares to his customers. In short, the uses of the cycle are numerous and varied, and will doubtless be added to.

Like all sports in their youth, cycling had its drawbacks and its dangers. The free use of the highways accorded to the velocipedestrian was in many cases grossly abused. Week after week, in the summer months, races at various distances, from one mile (?) upwards, were held upon the public roads, while several large organisations existed solely for the purpose of promoting road races. Public opinion was slowly but surely being roused to hostility by the course taken by a relatively small section of cyclists – the road-racing men, and the Jockey Club of cycling – the NCU failed to take the necessary steps to check the abuse, steps fully within the power of that body, until at length the police authorities were roused to action of a very drastic character, and preparations were made in the county of Huntingdon for the absolute stoppage of the North Road Club's 24 Hours Race. Had not that body at the last moment changed the course so as to avoid the county named, serious trouble would have followed. It is to be hoped that the road clubs will now definitely abandon their practice of racing on the highways, which can only result in serious curtailment of the privileges now enjoyed by cyclists on the road.

The sport is now fully and finally established in public favour, its organisation is approximately complete, it maintains a special press of a magnitude which astonishes an outside inquirer, its literature is extensive, and its popularity steadily extending. It is a sport which bids fair to be more international than national, albeit there can be no question that Great Britain, with its excellent roads, was and is the home of cycling.

2

Riding

Riding a bicycle is, for obvious reasons, more difficult than riding a tricycle. There are, however, points in common between the two classes of machine, and for this reason many of the instructions are equally applicable to either. Thus the directions with regard to pedalling, holding the handles, attitude when riding, etc., may all be applied with little, if any, variation to the tricyclist as well as the bicyclist.

The first necessity for the learner of the art of bicycle riding is a machine on which to make the early efforts – so well remembered by every active rider. In the earlier years the 'bone-shaker' as the original wooden bicycle was called, was the most useful machine to learn upon, but nowadays the rear-driving safety is almost universally adopted. In its earlier forms this machine was peculiarly 'tricky' as regards steering, the small front wheel and the angle at which the steering head was set being in the main the cause of this, but the safety of today steers steadily and well, and as the saddle can be dropped and the rider's feet brought well within reach of the ground, the difficulties and dangers experienced by the learner in his earlier struggles upon the original type are materially modified, if not entirely done away with. Machines suitable for the beginner's use – solid tired – can be purchased for £2 or £3.

The practical assistance and advice of a friend or attendant will go a great way to getting over the more serious preliminary difficulties of the work. Instructors are to be found in most big towns throughout the country. There are schools and agencies, where cycle riding is taught in a complete and satisfactory manner, and this is, without doubt, by far the best method of acquiring the art, for the attendants and instructors have had in most cases plenty of miscellaneous experience in the task which they undertake, and are thus enabled to bring their charges safely through the ordeal without any serious or unnecessary damage. Some pupils, of course, are more clumsy than others, and although much credit need not be given to the oft-told stories of men who simply take a bicycle, jump upon it, and ride off without any previous experience of the machine, yet, on the other hand, many cases occur in which a careful and painstaking instructor has taught a beginner to ride, mount, and dismount in three separate lessons of half an hour each. For this reason the would-be bicyclist should, if possible, go to a properly qualified teacher. The charges for instruction vary in different places, but a complete course, enabling the learner to mount, dismount, and ride sufficiently well, can generally be obtained for about half a guinea – while, if the learner decides to purchase a new machine of his teacher, instruction in its use will often be a part of the bargain.

It frequently happens, however, that the cyclist in posse does not reside near enough to any of the cycling academies to undergo the regular course of tuition, and is constrained to fall back upon his own resources to acquire the desired accomplishment, and, arduous as the task may appear, many men have triumphed in a very short time over all the difficulties which present themselves. As actual experience is always the best guide, it will be well to relate the course taken by a well-known rider, who taught himself enough in the course of a few hours to make bolder and more practical essay upon a convenient and quiet piece of road. Procuring a bone-shaker over which he could just stand, he took it into the garden, where on a level and smoothly kept lawn a horizontal bar had been erected. Standing beneath the bar, he, with its assistance, got across the machine with one pedal in a convenient position, and then, steeling himself for the effort, let go of the bar – which he had been firmly grasping with one hand – thrust wildly with his foot at the descending pedal, grasped the handle, and, shooting a couple of yards or so away from the bar, fell ignominiously sideways upon the turf, the small rosewood handle, owing to the weight of the clumsy vehicle, each time punching a neat hole about one inch and a half in diameter and three inches deep in the neatly kept lawn. These holes sorely puzzled the gardener next morning, and he was furbishing up his mole traps to capture the strange and destructive animal which had caused them, when he learned the truth.

These struggles went on for nearly three hours, off and on, a white stone being used to mark the farthest point reached until the whole length of the lawn was covered without a mishap, and the 'hill' at the other end (a grassy slope of about 8 feet) successfully surmounted. A modification of the same plan may be successfully adopted by the solitary learner. A stout rope stretched between two trees, the lintel of a conveniently placed doorway, or in fact any overhead point on which the learner can secure a firm hold, which will enable him to sit upon his machine, and place himself comfortably in position for a fair start, should either be devised or taken advantage of. Should the learner be able to secure the assistance of a practical friend, however, he will be very much better off, or two beginners can materially aid one another by following out carefully the suggestions and hints appended below.

Supposing them to have obtained a suitable machine, a cycle maker or repairer, or in default of these skilled workmen an ordinary blacksmith, should be got to run his eye over it so as to see that no serious defects or damages exist, and then the learners, if everything is right and the machine quite safe, can proceed to give one another lessons in turn. A few minutes at a time will be ample, say five or ten at the outside, and then the second man should take his turn, as at first the work is very exhausting and the tiro apparently goes backwards instead of progressing in the art. The running and walking beside the machine stretches the legs, and enables the dismounted man to recover himself by the time he is called upon to mount again. The saddle should be firmly fixed, great care being taken to see that it is even, and set straight. A saddle put on crookedly, or a little higher on one side than the other, will often mar a man's efforts to a serious extent when he is in the early stages of his task. Beginner number two should stand on the left of the machine, and grasp the handle firmly with his left hand, steadying it at the same time with his right. Beginner number one will then place his left foot upon the step, raise himself thereon, and seat himself in the saddle. The piece of road chosen should be slightly down-hill. The assistant should then hold the learner up on the machine, always doing his best to prevent his falling away from him, i.e. over to the right. The mounted man should not attempt to pedal at first, but should simply sit upright upon the saddle with a firm grip on the handles, and try his best to keep his balance by their use. The rule for steering is exceedingly simple, but its difficulty to the novice lies in the fact that, despite its extreme simplicity, it requires the rider to take instantaneously the exactly opposite course from that which his natural impulse suggests.

Supposing a rider feels himself falling to the right, the natural impulse will cause him to turn away from the direction of the threatened danger – a course which is instantaneously fatal, the rule, which is emphasised by italics, runs as follows: 'Turn the steering wheel towards the side to which the machine is falling'

For example, if the rider feels himself falling to the right, he should pull the right handle towards him, and push slightly at the left handle, then after a swerve or two, and a stagger towards a calamity on the opposite side, the balance is regained. Of course, at first there is a strong and natural tendency to overdo this corrective action, so that the beginner who turns his wheel sharply to the right to counteract an impending fall to the right finds himself the next moment falling to the left, owing to his having overdone this turn, and then, getting into a wild and flurried state, he naturally comes down. A capable and expert rider keeps his balance by following exactly the same rule, but the corrective turn of the wheel is infinitesimal, as the balance of the body of course co-operates to a very great extent in the maintenance of the equilibrium by means of the steering. The natural tendency of the beginner, as pointed out above, is always to turn his wheel the wrong way, so the attendant should keep on repeating to the rider the maxim, 'Turn the wheel towards the side to which you are falling'.

During all this time the mounted man should keep his feet off the pedals and concentrate all his attention on the steering, the attendant for the time being pushing him along at a fast walking pace, say 4 to 5 miles per hour. After a short time the rider will acquire the knack of steering sufficiently well to warrant his placing his feet on the pedals. This will momentarily upset all he has learnt. It is an admitted fact that practical tricyclists are by far the best subjects among the learners of bicycle riding, for they have acquired at least the knack of moving their feet in the rotary action, and are thus able to propel the machine without awkwardness even if they cannot balance it. The complete novice, on the other hand, as often as not pushes at the wrong time, awkwardly throws his weight on the ascending pedal, and frequently misses it, with, of course, disastrous results to his cuticle. A course of careful and intelligent tricycling (necessarily on a rotary-action machine) before beginning the initiatory stages of bicycling is for this reason most emphatically recommended.

The novice's two great difficulties will be found first in the steering, as detailed above, and then in the pedalling.

Having sufficiently mastered the art of propelling and steering the machine, the beginner will have to learn to mount and dismount, and here again the services of the assistant are very valuable. The most dangerous fall which a man can have is that which occurs at the moment of mounting or dismounting, as the sufferer not infrequently falls into, or on to, the machine, and very serious injuries may easily be inflicted by contact with the sharp angles of the frame, the edges of the step or the pedals, or with the handles. To learn to dismount, the rider, very carefully watched over by his friend, should begin a long curve to the left, so that the machine leans slightly to that – the getting-off – side, then reaching back carefully with the left foot, he should feel for the step, taking care not to put his toe among the spokes – which would of course result in a severe fall. Having found the step – and the assistant will do well to advise him by word of mouth in which direction to move his foot – he should rise upon it fairly at once, then throwing some of his weight upon the handles and the rest upon his left leg, turning the machine still more to the left and throwing more weight upon the left-hand handle, the rider drops easily and quickly to the ground. The dismount should be assiduously and carefully practised until the rider feels perfect confidence in the execution of the manoeuvre.

When this stage has been reached – and this is determined by the amount of practice the novice is able to give – he may go a step farther and learn to mount. This is most easily accomplished in the following manner: The beginner should practise a few dismounts on the lines laid down above. Then dwell for as long a time as possible on the step ere descending to the ground, until after a few experiments he finds he can stand on the step and keep the balance of the machine for several yards at a time. The next stage is to stand thus on the step, preferably on a slightly down-hill road, and while so doing to bend the left knee (holding firmly on to the handles at the same time) and just touch the ground with the right foot, immediately afterwards straightening the left knee and regaining the saddle. This exercise may be continued, with intervals for rest, until the rider feels quite confident of his own proficiency. And now comes the crucial test – that of mounting from the ground – a feat for which the above recommended exercises have gradually prepared the learner. On the oft-mentioned piece of slightly falling road, with the wind behind if possible, so as to make everything as easy as may be, the learner should place himself astride the rear wheel and put his left foot fairly on the step, the handles being firmly grasped, throwing most of the weight upon the left foot, several hops should be made with the right foot until a sufficient pace is attained. Then, holding well on to the handles, the left leg should be sharply straightened, and the rider should get into the saddle. This should prove an easy task after the necessary pace has been got up if the exercises set forth at length in the foregoing pages have been carefully and completely carried out.

At first, of course, from nervousness the beginner will be in a great hurry, but as soon as he gains confidence by frequently repeated executions of this movement, he should seek to perform it slowly and with the utmost care and deliberation. This caution is extremely necessary, for many bad habits and tricks are learnt in this stage of a cyclist's practical experiences, and many an otherwise good rider may be seen whose method of mounting a machine is simply ridiculous. One, for example, will get on to the step of his cycle with any amount of lightness and grace, and from that point spring into his saddle with a sort of jerky leap, which strains the spring and frame of the machine in a violent and perfectly unnecessary manner. Another may be noticed whose mounting is a painful and arduous undertaking, necessitating many struggles and entailing frequent failures. If the beginner will only take the trouble to study carefully the right way, he may hope to avoid the many faults of bad mounting.

It is well once more to emphasise the vital rule: *Do not hurry*. A very deliberate and careful mount may, by steady practice, be converted into an adequately rapid mount – sufficient for all practical purposes – which will always, with care, retain the very important quality of safety.

Mounting, riding, and dismounting having thus been explained, and, it is hoped, brought within the capacity of the beginner, he may at once begin to study the real art of bicycle riding as distinguished from what, for want of a better term, may be called the riding of the wheel by mere rule of thumb. The cyclist should from the first aspire to be something

more than a mere straight-away rider, he should seek to be a clever and expert master of his machine. For this reason, and with this object always in view, he should carefully study the various methods whereby he applies his power, should seek to acquire an effective, comfortable, and easy style, and to develop by careful and constant practice that dexterity of limb which is so necessary to pace. The cyclist is not recommended to take up that branch of the sport known as 'fancy riding.' Such tricks of balance may well be left to the circus performer and professional athlete, whose business it is to risk their limbs in these exercises and feats of skill. The average amateur cyclist should simply seek to acquaint himself with the qualities and peculiarities of the machine which he uses. The first point, when sufficient confidence has been gained by a course of steady and continual practice, is to try and acquire an easy, and, above all, comfortable style, and as this requisite is as indispensable to the tricyclist as to the bicyclist, the two classes may be taken under the one head. Readers will remark that an easy and graceful style is not spoken of, inasmuch as the latter cannot always be learnt, and the effort to gain it might is some cases prove an absolute drawback, for it may not be possible for a cyclist to be graceful and at the same time exert his full powers, just as in the same way many a first-class racehorse has not perfect action, and many a fast-running man has progressed in a most ugly style. In the same way man a good cyclist, in adopting an easy and comfortable attitude, suited to his individual idiosyncrasies, is often found to indulge in a habit which may be considered extremely awkward and ugly by the more hypercritical of the observers. A very sharp line must, however, be drawn between mere laziness as opposed to actual necessity, as very often the former is the true cause of the awkward style and clumsy action of many a young rider. The beginner should therefore seek to cultivate a style based on the very best models, and then, when his experiences are somewhat enlarged, he may modify it in one direction or another to suit himself, always of course taking care not to fall into any error whereby he may unnecessarily lose any of the good points which he has by careful practice acquired.

For ordinary road riding a fairly upright position should be assumed, although in ninety-nine cases out of a hundred the bolt upright attitude is as inconvenient in practical cycling

AWKWARD AND EASY.

as it would be in foot running, when the best efforts of the athlete are to be made. So the novice will bear in mind that when hurrying or riding against the wind, the body may be advantageously carried rather forward, always supposing that the handles and saddle have been rightly placed, and that the leg reach has been properly studied, of which more anon. This forward inclination of the body tends to throw most of the weight upon the pedals, and, when not exaggerated, it is most suitable, as it presents less surface to the wind. The position of the handles is a point which requires very careful consideration, as it very often happens that a mistake in this detail will permanently injure a rider's style. A very old and favourite theory with cyclists has been embodied in the oft-quoted phrase 'a straight pull', and handles have been put lower and lower to afford the rider the full advantage theoretically supposed to be thus obtained, until the extreme point of efficiency has been passed, and the style of the rider cramped and seriously damaged through his having to reach after his handles in a noticeable and consequently awkward manner. This is, in this connection, absolutely the most serious error that can be made, and the bicyclist would do better to ride with a short reach and bent arms rather than have the handles so low as to cause him to crane over with rounded shoulders to reach them, which very soon bows the back, pulls the shoulders forward, compresses the chest, and generally alters the comfortable pose and set of the body.

In the case of the tricyclist who suffers from a too lengthy arm reach the difficulties are less important, although they equally tend to spoil the style, added to which in the case of a well-poised machine the rider will find himself constantly slipping forward on to the peak of the saddle, and as constantly having to recover himself by raising himself on the pedals – an irksome and annoying task which can be at once obviated by altering the adjustment of the handles. A short arm reach, therefore, is very much to be preferred to an overlong one. The correct and most comfortable position of the arms can only be satisfactorily determined by actual experience and practice in each individual case, as the length of the arm is variable, but the best guide is to insure a slight flexion of the arm at the elbow when the handles are firmly held. This bending of the arm will insure an easy and comfortable position of the body and shoulders, and the rider's weight can in a moment be carried back by straightening the arms and throwing back the shoulders. These remarks, as will be seen, apply in a great measure to both bicyclists and tricyclists, but only a practical experiment can satisfactorily determine the exact and proper position of the handles on either class of machine.

When the proper height for the handle bars has been discovered, the correct angle for the handles themselves requires consideration. The best position is that which the hand takes most easily, but handles turned too much out are apt to cause the rider to spread his elbows and turn his shoulders forward. The best position is nearly parallel with the frame, and dropping slightly towards the ground. The handles should be held firmly, but not gripped with too much force, a fault much more common than most people would think.

When the preliminary stages have been passed the rider may begin to think of improving his style, and as a natural sequence his pace. One of the very first points is to understand and gradually acquire that mastery of pedal action – the art of ankle work – which makes all the difference between a good and an indifferent rider.

To clearly appreciate the point at issue – and this is of primary importance – let the rider seek the nearest grindstone or coffee mill, or in fact any apparatus fitted with a handle of the type usual in such machines. Taking hold of it, the experimentalist should move it to its highest point and then turn it slowly round, standing fairly behind, and, if possible, over it, so that the arm may be brought when straight in the position of the leg on a cycle, and he will find that the power he exerts can be roughly broken up into a series of direct forces. Supposing he is standing behind and a little above the grindstone, he first thrusts the handle away from him, the force being a forward horizontal one, roughly speaking. Then he presses it down, this being a downward vertical force. Then, before it quite reaches the lowest point, he begins to pull it towards him, exercising a backward horizontal force, and finally he lifts it over the relative dead centre, exercising an upward vertical force, and then commences the forward thrusting action again. Having carefully studied this action with the hand, the principle of keeping up the application of the power all round should be adapted, as far as possible, to the action of the feet when riding a cycle. It will be necessary to have a pair of shoes fitted to the pedals with deep slots, to give the feet the necessary grip and prevent their slipping, and if the machine can be placed on one of the 'home trainers' or otherwise raised from the ground so that the first ankle work may be done on a free wheel, the task will be all the easier. The theory will be best understood if the rider momentarily supposes that he has gone a few steps backward in the Darwinian line of human descent, and that he is once again quadrumanous or four-handed, after the style of our simian ancestors, his feet being replaced by hands. Were this four-handed being asked to sharpen an axe on a grindstone, he would probably grasp the conveniently arranged double handles of the grindstone with his nether hands, and perform the pull and thrust action illustrated above, while with his normal hands he held the blade he wished to sharpen. Supposing he had much of this exercise, a simian man would be likely to do exceedingly well upon a cycle, for, steadying himself upon the saddle with his normal hands on the handlebar, he would, with the others, grasp the pedals and not only push them down but pull them up, thrusting, pressing, pulling, and thrusting again in regular sequence. This would be practically the whole art of pedalling, and were man so formed as to be able to grasp as firmly with his feet as he does with his hands, his pace on the wheel would undoubtedly be greater. But the foot grip is wanting, and the next best plan must be looked for. This is supplied by a careful and intelligent cultivation of the use of the ankle joint, which by proper practice and constant exercise can be brought into a sufficiently skillful state to effect with consummate ease nearly all the various actions which a quadrumanous cyclist might perform, the main idea, as will have been gathered from the foregoing, being to exert throughout almost the whole revolution of the pedal a force or forces which shall tend to propel the machine, while ankle work, even in its weakest and least developed stage, prevents the rider from holding the pedal down when the lowest point is reached, a trick which very often has much to do with the notable slowness of a promising-looking rider. It is well therefore for the learner, as soon as he has mastered the rudiments of the art of riding, to begin to practise, however incompletely, the art of ankle work, as he will thereby modify and lighten his action and obtain a full return for all the exertions he may make.

It is a necessity in artistic ankle work that both legs should work equally, and the rider who begins to cultivate ankle pedalling is advised to begin the education of his left foot first. It is usually found that the left leg takes longer to acquire its full share of skill in this direction than the right. Sitting upon the machine placed as suggested upon some sort of stand, so that the driving wheel or wheels run free, or upon a 'home trainer', the rider should put the left foot upon the pedal, being careful to see that the pedal bars are fitted into the slots in the soles of the shoe. Then let the pedal drop to its lowest point, and from the stationary position start the wheel – using the left foot alone – by grasping downwards with the toes, raising the heel and bending the foot downwards from the ankle, and (to use the only expressive word available) 'clawing' the pedal backwards and upwards. This should be done fairly from a dead-stop half a dozen times, and then the break may be very lightly applied, and the same performance repeated. This course will initiate the beginner into the nature of the precise action required, and it must be carefully practised for a time both on the home trainer (if available), and also as far as the action is concerned in active riding on the road, until the knack or trick is fully mastered. Then, with a certain amount of break check on the trainer, or in the actual work out of doors, the rider should carefully carry out the following exercises, keeping them up as long as possible despite aches and pains (except cramp, which necessitates an instant dismount and a sharp friction of the muscles affected), so as to educate the joints and muscles up to the work required.

No rider can pedal properly in a week, only a very few are passably proficient in a month, while a master of the art takes years to develop, and never claims to be perfect, for not one man in a thousand can be found with equal power and equal action, so the beginner will see at once that he has plenty of scope for work and also for improvement. Constant, careful, and intelligent practice is not only absolutely necessary, but is the only way in which the thing can be fully mastered. At first a good deal of stiffness and some pain will be caused, especially in the knees, calves, and front of the shins, while the lower abdominal muscles are occasionally affected in common with those of the upper thigh, this is sometimes caused by overwork, or by attempting to practise up hill. A good embrocation can be recommended as a complete specific in such cases, but if the stiffness is very bad, warm fomentations or a warm bath may be taken, the embrocation being afterwards carefully applied, while after each spell of work the rider or his attendant should carefully rub the legs for 10 minutes or so with the bare hand, which will assist the circulation of the blood through the muscular tissues, and enable them the more rapidly to accommodate themselves to the novel task imposed upon them. As pointed out above, these exercises may be carried out upon any cycle or home trainer.

As suggested above, the left foot should first be carefully schooled (except, perhaps, in the case of those persons who are left-footed as well as left-handed), then the right, which latter should be put through the same exercises, though for a time less frequently than the left. As soon as some precision of action has been acquired, the learner should attempt a little slow and painstaking road riding, on a level road, not downhill or before the wind (as being likely to cause inadvisable rapidity), or up stiff hills or against heavy wind, because this will unduly tire the limbs and muscles. The right foot being taken off the pedal and put on the foot rest, or swung backwards, taking care, of course, not to get it in the spokes, the left should be carefully exercised alone, the machine being driven as straight as possible at a moderate pace. This strengthens and develops the muscles, and at the same time affords the rider or his attendant a practical opportunity of testing the actual amount of force exercised by the leg, a material point, as ankle action without a little power to back it is practically useless, albeit a very small amount of power can be made to go a very long way by the possessor of a good and well-studied ankle action. In fact, to this one accomplishment, possessed in a very high degree of efficiency, may without doubt be ascribed to some considerable extent the successes on the path and on the road of riders who, regarded merely from the muscular power standpoint, are by no means pre-eminently calculated to shine as athletes. As soon as the left limb has been fairly started, and has developed some little proficiency in the steady and even propulsion of the machine, that more promising pupil, the right leg, may be exercised in the same way, but care should always be taken, for months after the beginning of the work, not to forget the left leg, and not to throw all the labour – as so many riders unconsciously do – upon the right. The rider who follows out closely the above instructions will soon begin to appreciate the value of the art which he is acquiring, but he will do well to curb his impatience, and to adhere to his plan of daily practice at a slow pace for a considerable time. It is very bad policy to hurry, at any rate for some time after the rudiments of ankle action have been fully mastered, for if the rider gets up a high rate of speed he is almost certain to fall into some faults which will cause him to slur over some material portion of the stroke, it is therefore necessary that a rider who desires to gain a thoroughly irreproachable ankle action should devote daily a certain specified time to practising it at a slow pace, which may gradually be increased as proficiency is acquired, until at the highest speed of the racing path the all-round ankle action of the accomplished rider is seen in its highest development. While learning, say for the first couple of months, an exaggerated action is recommended, the heel dropped as low as possible, the toes alternately being pointed as high up and as low down as the ankle joint will permit, and the forward thrust and claw back carried out as far as possible. These actions, thus carried to the extreme, effect the same purpose as the skipping or jumping of the sprint runner: they stretch all the muscles and increase the freedom of motion in the joints, and thus assist materially in the development and freedom of the action, but when at length it has been fully mastered, and a lengthy practical experience has taught the rider that even at the highest speeds he does not slur or shirk the work, it is well to modify the action of the ankle as far as is compatible with the full use of the joint. The true art is to conceal art, and this modification properly learnt in no way impairs the effectiveness of the ankle action, in fact, it really increases its value by adding to its rapidity all round, and thus allows more scope for the use of the powerful muscles of the calf and thigh, while the easy smart rhythmic action of the ankle keeps the work alive, to use an expressive if somewhat technical metaphor. The real point is that the pull and thrust action, going on simultaneously with both feet, practically does away with the dead centre, and keeps the wheel running between the full throw strokes, a point which will be fully appreciated by all practical cyclists, and may be likened to that portion of the sculler's art which enables him to keep his boat running between the strokes. The rider must bear in mind throughout all his work that the downward thrust is of course his most valuable point, and that it should be fully taken advantage of, and not lost sight of in the course of the all-round action, but at the same time the quick clawing recovery prevents any hang of the machine at the dead point, and therefore materially aids propulsion. Nor is it right to suppose, as some riders have done, that ankle work is only of service on the racing path, and of no value elsewhere, as a matter of fact the very greatest value is to be attached to the art on the road. All our best road riders excel in a sound and straight ankle action. The road rider should therefore study and practise the art with as much care and assiduity as the racing man, as he will always find it of the greatest service in every branch of active cycling.

The next points that will require looking to will be the wheels themselves and their bearings, and the axles and bearings of tricycles. These may need a little screwing up, though the anxiety of the novice to do away with any side shake in his bicycle wheel is not to be encouraged, a very little looseness at this point does no harm, and shows that the bearings are not screwed up too tightly, while it often happens that to readjust the bearings of an old and well-worn machine causes the balls to break, owing doubtless to the alteration of the positions of the coned surfaces on which they run presenting some irregularity which has been worn there by constant and careless use. Obviously untrue wheels are necessarily unsafe to begin with, and also a serious detriment to the rider who desires to steer a straight and steady course, and thus it is always well to have such wheels at once put right by a competent repairer, who should be also asked to run his eye over the cranks and sec that they are straight. This fact being established, the pedals should be put on. These should be preferably rat traps which afford a good hold for the feet, and tend to prevent the rider from slipping his pedal. They should be true and straight, and if they are bought second hand they should be carefully examined. If any suspicion of untrueness is entertained the pins should be taken out and put between the centres of a lathe and rapidly rotated, when any bend will be easily detected, and may be at once put right, as a crooked pedal pin gives a very uncomfortable twist to the ankle joint, and very soon tires the rider, while constant use will give the cyclist a permanent bad habit of screwing with the foot, a most unfortunate trick, and one which causes the action to look particularly ugly. The step is useful on the safety, and many are well designed and fitted, others are of narrow shape and should be carefully watched, the edge being frequently rounded off with a file, as the constant friction sharpens it up to such an extent that it inflicts a very ugly wound should the rider be so unfortunate, from wet shoes or other cause, as to miss it in the hurry of mounting or dismounting. The teeth of the step, as well as of the rat-trap pedals, should also be kept moderately sharp, at any rate at first, until the rider has arrived at that stage of his experiences in which he recognizes the necessity of watching with care all these minor details of his steed's accessories, every one of which has a direct bearing upon his comfort and, what is still more important, his safety.

Accidents

Falls on the road or path are of course of occasional occurrence among cyclists. Although their frequency has been much exaggerated, a skillful rider will escape many an accident where an unskillful cyclist is certain to come to earth.

Many accidents are caused by the failure of some part of the machine, and are practically inevitable and unavoidable, beyond, of course, the exercise of a certain amount of care and supervision, an examination of all parts of the machine for cracks and flaws and so on will prevent many falls.

The habit of flying hills at a reckless pace, or runaways through inadequate break power, will often be found at the bottom of some of the most serious accidents on the wheel, and though caution may add to the time taken on the journey, it vastly improves the rider's chance of completing the trip in safety. A sound and well-fitted break is of course an essential to the road-riding cyclist. A stout pair of gloves is a great protection to the hands in the case of a fall, and when a cropper at high speed seems inevitable the rider should avoid as far as possible falling against banks or similar obstructions. A fair fall on the road, especially if the shoulder can be made to come first to the ground, generally results in a series of somersaults, which, though damaging to the cuticle and the angles of the frame, is not nearly so serious in its results as a dead stop against a bank or wall. It may seem absurd to offer hints how to fall, but it is quite an art of itself, for which many riders develop quite a peculiar talent. If the rider can by any little ingenuity twist or turn on to his back, the resulting injuries will be very slight. Should a rider fall on the road, as soon as the first pain has gone off he should essay to move. If his machine is uninjured and the cause of the accident clearly apparent, he should get on at once and make for the nearest doctor. If, on the other hand, he suspects a broken spring or a damaged bearing he will do well to walk, but in any case he should move off at once before his wounds get stiff. Careful bandaging and the application of Vaseline on lint will enable him to get home, and warm water and a soft sponge should be courageously employed to extract the grit and dust from the wounded surfaces, their subsequent treatment should be left in the hands of the doctor.

The path falls are decidedly the most serious in one respect, for if a rider has the misfortune to fall on cinders the results will be very disfiguring, blue marks exactly like tattoo and much of the same nature being the result when cinders are left in the wounds. Some of the best racing men have been sadly disfigured about the face, elbows, and knees in this way. It is therefore necessary for the rider or his friends to take instant action after an accident on the cinder path. Warm water if possible should be used, and the wounds superficially sponged over quickly to remove the surface cinder, then the edges of the wound, which resemble a series of parallel deep scratches, should be pulled gently apart, and the cinders which lie in them gently removed with the corner of a towel or a bit of sponge, frequent washing with water being necessary. The pain in some cases is considerable, in others the force of the blow temporarily dulls the nerves, and advantage should be taken of the fact. In cases of insensibility a similar course should be followed. On one occasion within our knowledge a friend seized a stiff nailbrush and brushed out a deep wound, with the double result of bringing the patient to his senses by the combined effect of pain and blood-letting and also of extracting all the cinder. Heroic remedies like these should, however, be gently used, under the eye of a doctor if by any means possible. Face wounds should always be well cared for, and the victim must be encouraged to permit the painful process as long as possible. If a companion will firmly grasp both wrists it will be found of assistance in the more painful moments. As in the case of road falls, Vaseline should be freely applied and a handkerchief tied round to prevent rubbing, and then the rider should be sent home as quickly as possible. Gentle fomentations with warm water will assist in keeping the wound open and extracting the foreign matter. Dr G. B. Partridge, of Anerley, in a letter on this subject says,

The best treatment undoubtedly is copious washing with warm water, it need not to be desperately hot, and much of the foreign matter may thus be got rid of with the aid of a soft rag or sponge. Very often larger fragments more or less embedded in the skin may be removed at the time with a needle point, and this will be a considerable gain as to speed of recovery, and subsequently large soft linseed meal poultices will materially hasten the separation of the particles too deeply embedded for such mechanical treatment. I do not think anything else can be done in aid of Nature's own process of cure, which is in itself fortunately a fairly rapid one, the superficial layers of the skin undergoing frequent removal.

Falls on the two most prominent surfaces used for cycle tracks today, wood and cement, require to some extent varying treatment. Wood being usually laid on a somewhat soft sub-surface, and being itself not extremely hard, gives slightly under the victim of the mishap, the wounds are clean and mostly straight cuts, and the rider only needs immediate attention as regards them. The man who falls upon cement is, however, less fortunate, and requires more care, as cement tracks are laid upon some inches of concrete to enable them to withstand the winter, and are of necessity extremely hard and unyielding. The actual wounds are no worse than those sustained by the man who falls upon wood, but the nervous shock to the system is infinitely greater. The after results are also more serious, and it is of the very greatest importance to keep this fact in mind in dealing with riders who have fallen heavily upon a cement track. Rest is a very great assistance to convalescence, and it is imperative in the worst cases. Of course broken bones need the surgeon's care, as also do more serious wounds than those alluded to above. The great thing is not to desire too rapid a recovery, and to give Nature time to re-establish the disintegrated membranes.

Cyclists, being usually in good health and fair condition, recover rapidly. There are numerous nostrums in the market, some of which are very successful in removing stillness, sprains, and bruises.

THE BRIGHTON COACH.

3

Dress

Exhilarating and enjoyable as is the sport of cycling, and healthy as it has proved itself to be, its enjoyment and its health-giving qualities are wholly dependent upon one very important point: a correct and suitable costume. It must not be forgotten that cycling is, after all, an athletic exercise, that it causes perspiration when ardently followed out, and for that reason alone it requires its votaries to be properly costumed in a dress suitable and convenient for the work in hand. It may be well to say a few words on this question of appropriate attire, as a good many riders are even now doubtful about the propriety of donning a regular cycling dress. In the earlier days of the sport, a pedestrian or a rider in cycling garb was sufficiently a novelty to attract a good deal of annoying attention in any town he might visit. But this is no longer the case, and a correctly dressed cyclist, more especially if he adopts the CTC costume, is so common an object, that he passes without special notice. One reason for the protection which ladies undoubtedly find in the CTC grey uniform lies in the fact that it is so little remarkable, and so closely resembles that ordinarily worn by the wife of the parson or doctor, and therefore the bucolic intelligence sets down the passing stranger in his mind as probably a friend or acquaintance of the local lady. Every day the public outside the sport become more and more used to the sight of a correctly dressed cyclist, and the familiar grey dress of the lady rider, and the knee-breeches, stockings, and short jackets of men, occasion no remark.

That every cyclist, of whatever age, should wear a cycling costume well-fitting and appropriately cut needs no proof. The rider of a cycle who ventures out in an inappropriate costume is regarded as one who does not know the right thing to do when pursuing the sport. The cyclist therefore should seek to be comfortably and scientifically clad, making the mere ornamental question as it affects the costume subservient to the necessity of having a practically useful dress in which to ride. The essential points are few and simple, they should be carefully studied by every cyclist who wishes to ride in comfort.

1. The dress must be fully protective – that is to say, it must afford an even and adequate warmth all over the body, without unduly confining the action of the limbs, and there must not be too much of it.
2. It must be of some very sound and serviceable cloth which can stand hard wear. Loosely woven cloth holds the dust, so the material chosen should be a wiry and closely woven stuff of some medium colour, and the costume as a whole should be neat and quiet in appearance. A practical

costume, meeting all the requirements of the rider, requires the experiences of many riders under varying conditions to bring it up to the point of practical perfection, and the ingenuity of cyclist after cyclist has been exercised on the many minor points which go to make it a complete and comfortable whole. Not only must the outer garments be suitable to the work and its surroundings, but the under garments must correspond. This remark applies with peculiar force to the clothing worn by ladies.

Outer Garments

These consist of the cycling costume proper, the coat or jacket, the waistcoat (if worn) the breeches or knickerbockers, the stockings, and the cap. No cheap material can withstand for any time the hard usage to which a cycling dress is of necessity subjected, and the truest economy is to pay a fair price for some tested material which experience has proved in every way suitable for the purpose.

The solitary cyclist might spend his life and a small fortune trying and testing various goods which would be highly recommended to him as suitable for cycling, and the lady rider would probably find that any garment which the shopkeeper had in stock was pronounced to be eminently adapted for her purpose. Happily for cyclists generally, expert assistance has long since been called in, and materials suited to all classes of riders are now supplied.

A cloth which specially finds acceptance among a large class of wheelmen is that sold by the Cyclists' Touring Club. It was originally decided upon by a jury of experts, who also fortunately happened to be cyclists. It is a West of England tweed, a very small check pattern in grey, it is excellent in wear, does not show the dust, and will stand any amount of knocking about, it will also wash, which is a great point, as a cyclist is apt occasionally to come in contact with oily parts of his machine. The CTC cloth, as it is usually termed, cleans remarkably well.

The material having been chosen, the make and shape must be decided upon, and here again experience has laid down certain principles which have been established by the slow process of discussion and trial. The result of these practical discussions has been the establishment of a few points as imperative rules for the comfort of the cyclist, and first and foremost stands the dictum: 'That every garment worn while cycling should be of flannel or woollen material, without any admixture of cotton or linen in any form.' The past experiences of many well-known and prominent riders in the early days of the sport taught them in the most emphatic manner, and sometimes with unpleasant emphasis, the imperative necessity of doing away with every atom of cotton or linen used in anyone of the garments worn, as these materials when damp from perspiration or rain are found to ' strike ' very cold and chilly, and this becomes more particularly apparent should the rider sit about after a hard day's work, when he feels chilled to the bone, and in many cases catches a very severe cold, if nothing worse, while some very bad cases of inflammation of the kidneys have been traced directly to the wearing of a linen waistband in the knickerbockers. As a number of elderly tricyclists will insist on riding in trousers, and will of course equally insist on wearing an old pair of an ordinary suit, they often suffer as above described, and cycling is blamed for an illness which can be directly traced to the folly of the victim himself. Sore throat is often to be traced to the linen band which so many tailors and shirt-makers will fit round the neck of a flannel shirt, while there is often in addition a little square of linen marked with the maker's name and address, which, when it is damp, can be readily felt, especially if the wind blows up coldly after a long run as evening falls. Throughout the whole list of garments used by cyclists the same fault extends, the merino or woollen vest has a strip of linen down the front right over the throat, and so placed as to be likely to produce the very worst results, the drawers, if worn, have a linen waistband and a linen front, the knee-breeches or knickerbockers are lined round the knees and at the waist with Italian cloth or some other 'cold' material, the coat is strengthened with a linen stiffener wherever necessary, and the arms are lined with linen or some kindred material. The waistcoat is backed with cotton and lined with cotton, and is altogether about as bad as it can be in this respect, seeing that the cold-giving material is stretched over the loins and round the stomach. The 'flannel' shirt, especially of the non-shrinkable and fancy class, contains a large proportion of cotton, and the result is that the rider after a long run is cold, clammy and chilly, loses his appetite instead of improving it, feels quite out of sorts, and may consider himself lucky if, in addition to all these discomforts, he does not get a heavy cold, or, worse still, a local chill. More especially is this likely to occur if the victim has a few hours of night riding at the finish of his day's work, when his only chance is to button his coat right up to the neck and keep moving until the very end of the trip, standing about, or trying to get warm by the fire, will only add to the chance of illness. On the other hand, the rider clothed from head to foot in complete flannel, or pure woollen garments, is comparatively safe

The 'body garment', the coat or jacket, is the first item to be considered, and there are plenty of designs and shapes to choose from. A jacket for bicycling should not be too long, but when the rider is seated upon the machine it should just reach below the saddle. For tricycling, and especially in the case of elderly riders who use an ordinary pattern front steerer, the jacket may be cut a little longer. The usual type, and one most popular with the general run of riders, may be described as follows: it should be single breasted, buttoning up with not too many buttons, it should be cut pretty high up round the throat, and fitted with a good wide lie-down collar, which should be finished in front with a small lappel, so arranged that when the collar is turned up the lappel may button across the throat. If a triangular 'tab' which can be buttoned across the opening of the turned-up collar be also fitted, and its lower corner hooked or buttoned over the lappel itself, it will be found a very complete protection for the throat and neck. The arms should be rather looser than ordinary, and the armholes cut a trifle larger to allow for extra garments at night and in the winter, and also to facilitate the putting on of the jacket over woollen underclothing. This enlargement should be very slight, not more than one inch at the most, but in actual practice this makes all the difference between comfort and discomfort. The sleeves should not be too long, or they will worry the rider very much, especially in case they get wet with rain or perspiration, and the cuffs should be fitted with a couple of buttons so that they may be opened and turned back in hot weather. For winter use the coat may belined throughout with thin sound flannel, but in the summer this will be found oppressive unless very little underclothing is worn. For a summer jacket the very smallest amount of lining and stiffening, which should invariably be all of woollen material, should be used.

Next in order of merit as a useful garment for ordinary wear comes the 'Norfolk jacket'. This shape is well known to most sportsmen, it is light and easy, and commends itself particularly to those who are inclined to be stout. The same rules, as far as cut and make go, will apply to this jacket, it should be made to fit loosely, and the belt should be fixed to the jacket above the hips, the pockets are usually put in the breast folds, and when the Norfolk jacket is made in CTC cloth it looks exceedingly well. It is particularly suitable for couples riding tandems, as it is a type of jacket which suits many ladies excellently, and the couple being in the same cut of jacket undoubtedly adds to the neatness of the turn-out. The waistcoat is a thing not much worn by active cyclists, although the tourist will in many cases find it a most useful addition to his outfit. There is nothing special about it except that it should be cut high, in fact the square clerical cut may be best adopted. The back and lining of such a waistcoat should always be of flannel, and need not be so heavy as it is ordinarily made. A combination garment has been suggested, an all-cloth waistcoat fitted with arms and cut a trifle longer than usual, a sleeveless coat to be put on over it, which, when the rider gets out into the country, could be taken off and easily packed away. The idea seems practical, and might be adopted.

Either knickerbockers, knee-breeches, or trousers may be worn, the taste and fancy of the rider being left to settle this question. Trousers, however, are certainly the least suitable, as having no support at the knee they are sure to slip downwards and drag, while any scheme for looping them up or fixing them, though it may affect its object so far as to allow the rider to use the machine without fear of accident, invariably makes them look awkward and uncomfortable.

Knickerbockers require careful cutting to look well. Flannel linings should be used throughout, the garments should be very carefully fitted, and not cut too high. They are best fastened with a cloth strap and buckle at the knee, which should not be drawn too tight, they should be made with a view to the position assumed by the rider when on his machine.

In all cases the breeches should be worn well braced up, so as not to hang in a loose and baggy manner. On the other hand, too tight bracing up will cause endless discomfort, and induce the cyclist to stoop in an awkward and constrained position.

Pockets in the breeches are not much recommended, but if they are adopted they are best placed high up in front, close under the brace buttons, and they should not be too large. A side-seam pocket is apt to gape when the rider is mounted, and unless made very deep, and consequently awkward to get at, the articles contained in it are liable to be lost. If the rider wears a loosely cut jacket, say a Norfolk jacket, a breeches pocket on the back of the hip is a very good addition. If there be no watch pocket in the jacket, it can be very comfortably added to the breeches, put close up to one of the brace buttons, and having a hole in front of the pocket to pass the chain through.

There are several very dangerous ideas which some practical riders have adopted, thus one rider has a long pocket just inside the opening of his jacket in which he carries an adjustable spanner. Were he to fall heavily on his chest, the chances are that this spanner would break one of his ribs, or inflict more serious injuries. The same remark applies to those riders who carry a bell or pump in their breast pocket when not in use. An inner pocket can be made in fully lined garments inside the right breast to take the CTC ticket, but overloading a suit with pockets inevitably spoils its look, and eventually its shape, so it should be avoided as far as possible.

Possibly it may not strike a casual observer that there could be much variety in the matter of stockings, but the ingenuity of hosiery manufacturers has supplied the cycling world with a pretty extensive choice in this important item. Well-fitting leg gear is an essential in the outfit of a rider. The most usual error into which cyclists, as well as manufacturers, fall, is the wearing or making of too long stockings. Thus stockings reaching halfway up the thigh have been offered as suitable for cycling, whereas the less stocking a rider can wear with comfort and decency the better, always supposing that the breeches or knickerbockers are neatly cut, and reach, as they should do, well below the knee. Some of the more elaborate double-kneed arrangements are hot, heavy, clumsy, and decidedly uncomfortable, while they seriously interfere with the free action of the knee joints, and should be avoided. If adequate arrangements are made for holding the stocking up, the less strained it is the better, so long as it does not fall into creases or folds. For all-round wear an ordinary fairly stout ribbed stocking will be found the best.

In the case of new stockings, put on for the first time, it is an excellent plan to soap the joins and edges carefully with a piece of common yellow soap, as this will prevent the stocking from rubbing the foot in any part, and abrading the skin. Attention to this little point will often save a rider hours of painful work. In the summer time, and for short runs, a much thinner stocking may be worn. Thread stockings are on no account to be recommended. The tourist should adhere rigidly to wool, and wear fairly-stout stockings of that material.

The great question with all stocking wearers at all times has been how to hold them up, as although a new pair if well-made will cling to the limb, and look smooth and neat, as soon as they are a little worn and loose they will slip down and look very bad indeed.

The various slings and kindred arrangements are by no means suitable for the use of cyclists, as they are arranged for the upright position of a man when standing, and are not a success when used by a rider in active work, moreover, most of them merely transfer the drag from the knee to the waist or shoulder, and they are therefore to be avoided. The constant motion, too, causes the metal clips or fastenings to rub the skin, thus setting up an annoying soreness, and in some cases causing worse troubles. The garter, though by no means wholly satisfactory, seems to be the only practical plan. Non-elastic garters should in no case be worn. The slight drag of the stocking causes the hard and unyielding garter to press tightly upon the muscles and vessels at the top of the calf, and may give rise to varicose veins. Some of the spiral wire arrangements, if carefully adjusted so as to be exactly the right length and no less, are very good, as the slight gaps between the wires permit circulation, and are more likely, when in action, to shift a little, so as to alter the points upon which the pressure comes. The most frequent error in using these garters is having them much too tight, and this should be most carefully avoided. The broad-flat elastic garter made for ladies' use is fairly good, but the buckle or latching arrangement is altogether too elaborate, and might possibly cause a severe injury if driven into the leg, in the event of a fall. After a careful testing of every contrivance in the market, it is probable that the practical cyclist will eventually come back to the original plan of a plain broad elastic garter, which, if carefully made, will be found the most comfortable and serviceable.

Double heels and toes are a mistake in cycling stockings, and in fact in stockings used in any athletic sport, as the double portions have a very marked 'tendency to stretch unequally, with the obvious result that they go into rucks and creases, and cause endless trouble. There should be little or no actual friction, that is if a well-fitting shoe be worn, properly laced up over a well-fitting stocking. The main idea in all sorts of cycling work is to allow the foot plenty of play, and to keep it as cool as possible.

The next point to be considered in the outer garments is the head gear, and here again the individual fancy of the rider must be consulted. The wide-awake, deer stalker, and other hats of this class, will be found of more general service than any others. A wide brim is an essential in a cycling hat, and it should also be light, ventilated, and durable. If a felt be chosen, it should be a soft one, of a colour either matching the coat worn, or very distinct from it. Some of the lighter greys and browns are very suitable for summer touring. They should have a moderately high crown, which should be fully ventilated by means of a number of metal-edged eyelet holes, and a hat-guard is a necessity, as if the hat is crammed on tight, when the wind is blowing it is almost certain to cause headache and similar troubles. The brim should be wide, but not too wide. It should be just stiff enough to retain its shape against an ordinary breeze, as to have one's hat brim flapping over one's eyes, perhaps when halfway down a hill, or at any other similarly awkward time, is troublesome or even dangerous. For winter riding a plain black felt wideawake may be recommended. A high-crowned hard felt affords a very great protection from the rays of the sun, though it is hardly so useful in wet weather, and catches the dust. The helmet is perhaps the very best head gear for touring work in all weathers. In this alone will be found those proper provisions for complete ventilation which are usually so conspicuous by their absence in ordinary hats and caps, while the protection afforded to the nape of the neck, and the freely ventilated space between the top of the head and the top of the helmet, are all of the greatest value to the rider who goes a-cycling in the hot sun of summer. Except in the hottest weather the neat, light and comfortable cricket cap may be worn with safety and comfort, and its use is daily becoming more universal. The cap should be of flannel, unlined, and with a stiff peak also of flannel, which may be stiffened with a piece of leather not too thick. This cap has many points to recommend it for ordinary wear, it is very light, fully ventilated, seeing that it is of thin and very open flannel, without lining. The peak affords protection to the eyes, and can be turned round to shade the back of the neck, while it should never be lost, seeing that it can be rolled up and put in the pocket with ease.

The great question of boots *v.* shoes was for a long time debated, but time, which settles all things, has most decidedly settled this question in favour of shoes. At one time a theory was strongly advanced that it was necessary to wear boots to support the ankle, and the sport of skating was adduced as evidence of the necessity of that support being given. It did not occur to the advocates of the boot side of the argument that on a cycle the bodily weight of the individual was carried by the machine, and that the muscles which carried the body in ordinary case were, whether strong or weak, available for the support of the ankles and the propulsion of the machine, added to which the tendency of the pedalling was to keep the foot and ankle straight, and the theory of support for the ankle was thus absolutely negatived by facts. It is interesting when considering this fact to remember that medical men are now prescribing tricycle exercise for children who suffer from weak joints, either at the knee or ankle, as they find that as the weight of the body is not thrown upon the joints, the exercise they thus obtain tends gradually to strengthen them. The theory that weak joints require support for cycling work is consequently untenable, and those who are victims of this evil will do well to undergo a short course of tricycle or bicycle exercise, which will strengthen the muscles and joints without the otherwise unavoidable strain of the bodily weight upon the tender parts.

Foot gear, however, to return from this digression, becomes simply a question as to what shoes shall be worn, and it will be well to consider the uses to which the foot is put. It is an absolute necessity that the foot should be free to extend itself and to carry out untrammelled all the varied actions described in the foregoing chapters on ankle action and pedaling generally. To secure this desideratum the shoe must be light, flexible, and easy. The sole, too, must be of sufficient thickness to preserve the bottom of the foot from feeling the bars of the pedals, and should be as stiff as possible, as in this case the rider practically gets the whole surface of the sole whereon to apply his power, instead of having to push at two narrow bars of iron. The sole of the shoe may with advantage have a piece of steel run up the middle, that is the middle of the front sole from the waist to the toe, not from the waist to the heel. This piece of steel should be flat and broad, and it will be found of the very greatest assistance in keeping the sole flat, and thus precluding in most cases the possibility of cramp in the toe joints, especially in the joint of the great toe. The rider should be very careful to see that the shoemaker uses a flat piece of steel, as many tradesmen, to save themselves trouble, will use a bent waist spring, which in time invariably bends the sole very awkwardly.

Thus far the outer garments suitable for men, the larger section of cyclists, have been described, but before passing to the next section it will be well to say a few words as to ladies' dress for cycling purposes, and it is also advisable to note that in the main the divergence between the appropriate cycling costume of the two sexes is confined solely to the outer garments, as the under-wear is of necessity very similar in either case, ladies having taken advantage of the experiences gained by their husbands and brothers, and adopted with but slight modification the underclothing which they have found most suitable for use while indulging in the sport. A well-designed costume will allow of the greatest freedom of action, and thus enable its wearer to ride a machine without the troublesome and tiring drag which is always felt if an ordinarily dressed woman mounts a velocipede. On the other hand, the would-be dress reformers seized upon these undoubted facts and desired to use the tricycling ladies as a medium whereby they might introduce to the public their crude notions of a suitable and hygienic dress. Seeing that the spectacle of a lady on a tricycle was at that time a novelty sure to attract remark, it was somewhat unreasonable that those who were courageous enough to ride should be asked to render themselves doubly conspicuous by putting on a novel and outré costume. But although the reform was not adopted in its entirety, the ladies interested took up the question, and at a meeting called by the CTC the matter was carefully discussed, the following decisions, which embody a full description of a cycling dress for ladies, being arrived at:

A lady who dresses from a practical hygienic point of view invariably discards the majority of the garments usually worn, and assumes those more in consonance with the taking of healthy athletic exercise, with its concomitant need of freedom of movement – the result being that the few articles assumed have to compensate for the inevitable loss of warmth which must otherwise ensue. The uniform strongly recommended embraces the following:

1. A combination merino or woollen garment to be worn next to the body.
2. A pair of dark grey woollen or merino stockings.
3. A pair of loose knickerbockers, of the Club cloth, fastened with elastic, or by a cloth strap and buckle, under the knee, to be suspended from the hips or the shoulders at the option of the wearer.
4. A pair of trousers cut loose to just below the knee, and thence tighter just down to the foot, to be suspended from the hips or shoulders at the option of the wearer.
5. A plain skirt, of the club cloth, without kilting, and of sufficient fullness to admit of absolute freedom of movement without undue bulk.
6. A bodice or jacket, at option of wearer, cut either to fit the figure, or of 'Norfolk' shape, lined throughout (including sleeves) with the Club flannel, and provided with an adjustable belt if so desired.
7. A helmet or hat of the club cloth, or of straw, with a special and registered ribbon, in any of the shapes that may be provided by the Club from time to time.
8. A pair of soft 'Tilbury' doeskin gloves.

This costume embodies all the necessary points of a hygienic riding costume. The cloth should be closely woven and not fluffy or rough, as in either of these cases it will hold the dust and defy brushing, neither should it be too thick or too heavy, and it should be neither too light nor too dark in colour, a happy grey medium being undoubtedly the most serviceable. That ladies generally will be fully competent to suit themselves in this matter there can be little doubt. As with the bicyclists' costume, the ladies' cycling dress was not designed at once, but was gradually perfected by active riders in constant work. The all-flannel, or rather the all-woollen, costume is even of more moment in this case, as the danger of colds is possibly greater with those who do not so frequently indulge in exercise, and no rider should wear anything but wool. One drawback which has existed for some time in this connection has now been removed, as all-wool corsets are obtainable as well as every other requisite for a lady's cycling costume.

The choice of a body garment is not a difficult one, but unfortunately lady riders are very fond of a tight-fitting bodice or jacket, which, however well it may look, must of necessity be hot and uncomfortable, and a tight jacket should be carefully avoided if the rider means to ride in earnest and not to play at cycling. Of all the different styles of jackets, nothing touches the Norfolk jacket for all-round use. If nicely cut it looks well, is comfortable, and appropriate, and as it can be worn by either sex, it is a most serviceable garb. In all material points, the instructions laid down for cutting the ordinary Norfolk jacket should be observed. Some of the closer fitting jackets with a military collar are suitable for cold weather.

When ladies first began to ride they were constrained by prejudice to ride upon a seat placed low down and some distance behind the pedals, and this position, besides being awkward and uncomfortable, was also exceedingly dangerous. The dress in this case was constantly getting up over the knees, each alternate stroke lifting it higher, and many attempts were made to design some method of keeping it in place. Some riders sewed a considerable weight of shot into the lower edge so as to keep it down, while others fastened the front of the skirt to the front of their boots or shoes, with the very obvious result that the skirt dragged tremendously over the knees and rapidly tired the rider. Many cyclists of both sexes made experiments to see how best to overcome this serious difficulty, and a remedy was found, although not quite in the direction anticipated. Instead of altering the dress, it was the position of the rider which was altered, instead of sitting low down, and a long way behind the pedals, she was placed upright and well over the pedals. At first many ladies so placed insisted on still using the seat instead of the saddle on the tricycle, and were proportionately uncomfortable, but in due time they were converted to the use of the saddle, and at once found their troubles were over. The knees, instead of awkwardly rising and falling in front of the body, were merely moved in a manner closely resembling the action of walking. The skirt was simply thrown out by either knee alternately, and still hung gracefully and comfortably in front of the rider. This was the solution of a difficulty which bade fair at one time to prevent many ladies from following the sport.

The skirt should be just long enough for walking purposes, and no more. It should be of sufficient size to admit of the freest motion of the knees, and made of some closely woven and wiry material which will not cling unduly to the figure. It may be a part of the jacket, or may be worn with a belt or suspended from one of the under garments, the latter plan being the best, as doing away with any tight cinctures around the body. It should be simple in design and not loaded with braiding.

On the question of the head dress the ladies may freely exercise their own choice, but in general a smallish hat is advisable, with some provision for the adequate protection of the neck and eyes. With the general caution not to have too large a hat to catch the wind, or too small a one, which would not afford adequate protection from the sun, this point can be dismissed. Ladies will of course adopt shoes when riding, and these should be light and of thin leather, with a thin waist as flexible as possible. Eyelet holes should replace the hooks which the bicyclist is advised to adopt, as the latter catch in the front of the dress and tear it, besides sometimes tripping up the rider from a similar cause. The shoe should open a good way down, and if it is neatly made this will cause the foot to look all the smaller and be of great service to the wearer. The steel in the sole is not an absolute necessity, but should any lady rider suffer from cramp, or be continually missing her pedal, a steel and grooves to take the rat-trap pedals should at once be fitted, as this will enable her to keep her foot straight, and at the same time will correct the error into which she has fallen. The garments worn under the skirt may be practically regarded as outer garments, as they are usually made of the same cloth and assimilated as much as possible to it. A choice is offered between trousers and knickerbockers, but the latter are much to be preferred, as trousers will inevitably drag very much over the knees and fatigue the rider. A carefully fitted pair of knickerbockers, with a cloth strap and buckle at the knee, will be found the most useful garments to wear under the skirt, and if the stockings be either of some dark colour or else match the dress, and the skirt be cut the right length, it will both look well and prove comfortable, regarded merely as a cycling costume. Here again it is scarcely necessary to point out that ladies should go to a practical ladies' tailor for cycling clothes, as unless the maker is aware of the particular purpose for which they are wanted, and has some special knowledge of the requirements of the case, the garments when made will not be likely to prove successful. The latest development in cycling costume for ladies is that styled 'Rational', the rider wearing knickerbockers and gaiters and a long-skirted jacket. It is claimed that if ladies are to ride at all, they should ride as comfortably, safely, and easily as possible, and the new dress enables them to use a safety bicycle with a top stay to the frame, which makes a most marked difference in the ease and comfort of the machine, while the safety secured by the absence of the skirt is immense.

The final maxims therefore are:

1. Wear nothing but pure woollen garments.
2. Have them cut by a practical cycling tailor.
3. Study the even distribution of warmth.

4. Do not over-clothe the body.
5. In the event of a longish ride, always take a dry under vest in case of accidents.

By following out the above few precepts, the cyclist, lady or gentleman, will be enabled to ride in comfort and safety, whatever may be the state of the weather, throughout the year.

Cycling for Ladies

It would be difficult, at this date, to determine with any hope of accuracy who was the first woman courageous and enlightened enough to insist upon sharing a sport which had begun to prove itself of such pleasure and benefit to men. Certainly, in 1878 there were rumours of a lady cyclist who had accompanied her husband in an extended tour, and, despite some public consternation and criticism, women were here and there, all over the country, beginning to take more or less furtive rides on the machines of their male friends and relations. Once they had tried the sport, the taste for it seized them with full force, and it is a remarkable testimony to the charms and advantages of cycling that they made themselves recognised by women, through all the terrible drawbacks with which feminine cycling was handicapped in its initial stages. At first there were no ladies' cycles at all to be bought. A woman was compelled to make her first essays on a man's tricycle, too heavy for her, and dangerous and unsuitable in every way. As cycling began to grow in popularity with woman, an attempt was blunderingly made to supply machines for her special use. These were grotesque in their unsuitability to her needs. Brakes were inadequate, steering was awkward and leisurely, an inconvenient cushioned seat took the place of a saddle, and neither pace, safety, nor did comfort attend the clumsy, over-heavy, unwieldy tricycle on which she was supposed to taste the pleasures of the sport. Yet, in spite of these drawbacks, and of the fact that the ordinary costume worn by women is dangerous and most unsuitable to cycling, there was a slow but steady increase in the number of lady cyclists throughout this country, for years before the women of any other nation had been tempted to follow the example of their English sisters.

It is little wonder, considering all things that at first medical men, themselves without any practical knowledge of cycling, strongly warned women not to indulge in it. But women liked cycling too well to be frightened from it. They began to discard seats for saddles, to demand lighter mounts and a possibility of speed. When handlebars and bicycling steering were first applied to ladies' machines, there was an outcry against so mannish an innovation, but the result was an enormously increased popularity of the sport, and from that time makers seriously turned their best attention to catering for women's needs.

Ladies' cycles have now reached something like perfection. Light, elegant, safe and swift, supplied with strong brakes and efficient dress-guards, they place their riders on an equal plane of advantage with men. The old cry of warning that cycling was injurious to women has long since died out, and physicians strongly advocate it as the best exercise ever invented for the sex, with common-sense limitations. The army of cycling women throughout Europe and America is immense, and increases yearly. It is difficult, in these later days, for novices to realise how great was the struggle pioneer women had to make for their liberty to ride at all, and they should not forget to be grateful for the perseverance, courage, and good sense which paved the way now made so easy.

For a good many years the tricycle was a woman's only mount. The mere suggestion of a bicycle in connection with feminine use was thought shocking. The first idea of such a revolution came about through the introduction of tandem bicycles, where a lady was induced to take the front seat under masculine convoy and protection. Gradually a few two-wheeled machines for ladies' use appeared, and once more protests were universal. Six years ago, a woman on a bicycle was regarded as a curious and unedifying spectacle, women learned to ride in their own secluded gardens, or in the early morning, when no spectators were abroad. But the undoubted advantages of the new mount began at once to assert themselves, and it has long since almost entirely ousted its three-wheeled rival from the field of feminine use.

The Ladies' Tricycle: This should be light in weight, and furnished with inflated tyres. It should have a strong and effective break, fitted preferably with a double lever, the spring should be carefully calculated to the rider's weight, the saddle should be carefully chosen, and neither too large nor too small, the dress-guard should be complete, and the construction of the frame such as to allow ample room for drapery, if worn.

The advantage of the tricycle is that the rider can remain in the saddle while at rest, and that a feeling of security is imparted, very valuable to the elderly or nervous rider. This is its only merit unshared by the two-wheeler. Against it may be quoted a list of inherent and ineradicable disadvantages, which are as follows:

1. Its weight.
2. The greater exertion involved in propulsion.
3. The impossibility of dismounting when moving.
4. The three tracks.
5. The lateral jars and twists.

The extra weight is a very serious consideration, and so is the greater effort involved. These make the tricycle a more fatiguing mount than the bicycle. Dismounting is a somewhat awkward performance, having to be accomplished from the front of the machine, not over the axle. The three tracks make it an inconvenient mount on bad or newly metalled roads. A serious drawback lies in the fact that one of the three wheels may be thrown up higher than the others, thus conveying a jar or twist to the rider.

The Lady's Safety: The only disadvantage of the rear-driving safety as a lady's mount lies in the necessity of keeping the balance. How small this difficulty is, and how readily overcome, will at once be proved by the hundreds of women who learn in a few lessons, and the extraordinarily small number of accidents to feminine bicyclists. Skill is of so much more importance in the matter than physical strength, that a woman has points in her favour in the matter, it being an acknowledged fact that where skill and aptitude in learning are concerned the average woman has an advantage over the average man. The special points of advantage possessed by the rear-driving safety are as follows:

1. It is lighter than a tricycle, has fewer working parts and no balance gear, and therefore is more easily driven.
2. The method of mounting is much simpler, easier, and more graceful than the tricycle mount.
3. The method of dismounting is as easy, even while the machine is in motion.
4. The machine makes but one track, a most important point, as it enables the rider to pick her way along bad roads where a tricyclist would be forced to dismount.
5. The absence of any lateral jars or twists, any obstruction being encountered in the central line of the machine.
6. The possibility of applying adequate and ample brake-power, if necessary, to both wheels.
7. The increase of speed.

The safety, it will therefore at once be seen, is immeasurably superior to the tricycle. It is also quite as free from danger, if not more free, when ridden at the same rate of speed. If a lady is thrown from a tricycle, it is almost impossible for her to fall upon her feet, as the driving wheels are in the way, and a free escape would be impossible. On the other hand, in the case of a side slip, or any similar accident, on a safety, the chances are very much in favour of the rider alighting on her feet.

The method of mounting is simplicity itself, and can be acquired in one lesson. The rider stands on the left side of the cycle, holding the handles firmly, and inclining the machine slightly to the left. The right-hand pedal is brought to the front about two inches, and the rider puts her right foot firmly upon it. Then simply springing from the ground off her left foot, she rests her weight partly on the pedal and partly on the handles, and seats herself with the greatest ease in the saddle. Though at first hurried, before the rider has quite mastered it, this mount, when once perfectly acquired, is deliberate and graceful, much more simple and graceful than the lady tricyclist's mount. The dismount, also, is simplicity itself, the rider merely stepping out on either side of the machine at pleasure. The adjustment of a lady's safety is of great importance, as upon it depends both her comfort and success as a cyclist. If the rider can sit upon the saddle without holding the handles or touching the pedals, and does not feel a tendency to slip either backwards or forwards when sitting upright, the adjustment is correct. The front of the saddle should be from 3 to 4 inches behind a vertical line drawn through the centre of the crank axle, and it should not be put too high, as a full reach will be found very irksome, and will also interfere with the ankle action. The handles should be brought well within the rider's reach – this is most important. The arms should be just bent when the rider is sitting up. If the handles are placed too low and too far away, the position becomes most unsuitable. Some women affect the crouching attitude when on a bicycle. The effect is injurious to their health, and hideously ungainly to the eye of the spectator.

The ladies' safety should have smallish wheels with inflated tires. Ample brake power should be fitted, preferably with two levers. The work should be put low, but the pedals should not come too near the ground. The chain should be well protected by an adequate chain-guard, and the driving wheel may with advantage also be covered with a guard, if care be taken to give plenty of clearance inside the guard and in the forks.

An auxiliary foot-brake, distinct from the other, and preferably working on the back wheel, is a great addition. The lamp holder should project from below the footrest on the right-hand side, as being more out of the way. A fair amount of luggage can be carried on the safety when touring.

Tandem bicycles and tricycles are still used where a woman feels the necessity of masculine strength as an aid in riding, or prefers close companionship and escort to the greater independence of a mount of her own. They will always preserve a certain measure of convenience, probably, as family machines, though they are by no means popular to the extent that they were in their first youth.

The greatest revolution in feminine cycling that has taken place since its first days is undoubtedly the introduction of 'rational' dress. This originated on the Continent in 1893, and with it a sudden leap of cycling into feminine favour took place. The one drawback to the pleasurable cultivation of the sport by women has always been the discomfort, danger, and indecorum of the ordinary long skirt in connection with wheels. Almost every accident which has ever happened to women while cycling has been caused by the entanglement of their draperies, an occurrence against which it was impossible entirely to guard, no matter what precautions were taken. The fatigue of riding in a costume whose weight and friction were felt with every turn of the pedal, and which formed an obstruction to progress in any strength of wind, cannot be realised by those who have never suffered under it, while the mind of woman was perpetually disquieted within her over futile contrivances for keeping her floating skirt within the limits of seemly appearance. Some bold spirit seized and adopted the idea of discarding the long skirt altogether, and supplying its place with a neat and suitable costume of knickerbockers, long leggings, and a coat or tunic sufficiently long to add a feminine touch, while in no way interfering with free movement. As soon as the new dress was seen abroad, it was enthusiastically adopted. Cycling at once became a fashionable craze among Frenchwomen, and smart society began to take it up everywhere. The costume found its way to England in the same year, and, despite some vehement and slightly unreasoning prejudice on the part of a certain section of the public, it made rapid headway in general favour.

There is no doubt that, however much its novelty may have caused surprise, the advantages of the new costume are overwhelming. It has at once removed the ever present element of risk from the entanglement of draperies, it is a thousand times more decorous than the unmanageable, fly-away skirt, it gives women a chance of riding at an equal advantage with men in point of ease and comfort. There is another enormous point in its favour. To accommodate feminine draperies, the whole framework of the safety had to be altered, in supplying mounts for their use. The frame was dropped in a U or V shape, which so weakened it that expedients of double tubing and stays inserted low down had to be resorted to, in order to make it fit to support any strain. With all these contrivances, it remained far inferior in strength and stability to a man's mount, and it was impossible that it should be otherwise.

But 'rational' dress entirely obviates the necessity of the dropped frame, and puts a machine of ordinary construction within the riding capacities of any woman.

Whatever may be urged in favour of cycling as a health-giving exercise for men may be repeated with redoubled force when the pastime is advocated for women. The majority of small illnesses common among women arise from disordered nerves and digestion, brought on by lack of fresh air, regular exercise, and an interest outside of domestic concerns. Cycling is a panacea for all these. The effect upon low spirits, general 'little health', and feelings of constant misery and discomfort, can be testified to by countless women today. To many lives, narrowed down to petty household cares and interests, it has brought fresh zest and amusement. As a factor in the existence of women and girls its benefits are incalculable.

As an instance of the rapid growth and power of feminine cycling, it may be mentioned that it has been found necessary to legislate for feminine interests. The Lady Cyclists' Association of Great Britain, founded in 1892, rapidly became an organisation of such importance that delegates from it were accepted by the NCU, and it was acknowledged to be the most powerful promoter in existence of reform in matters connected with feminine cycling. Its firm defence and patronage of 'Rational' dress was one of the strongest aids dress reform had ever had brought to back it up in this country, and its discouragement of cycle racing by women strongly showed how the movement was condemned by the majority of women who ride.

Medical authorities agree in saying that the strain of training for a cycle race cannot fail to be injurious, not only to any woman indulging in it, but to the race at large. The L.C.A., recognising this fact, and the injury that the spread of racing was likely to do feminine cycling, took a strong stand against its increase. Had it been foretold, in the first days of the pastime, that women cyclists would ever be in a position to form an organisation powerful enough to effect any action in a matter that chiefly concerned themselves, the prediction would have been received with incredulity.

At the present time, in even the most remote parts of the kingdom, the sight of a woman on a bicycle has ceased to attract attention. Wearers of 'rational' dress have made long tours throughout the country, entirely unattended, and have received neither uncourteous notice nor annoyance. The prejudices which existed against cycling for women have long been seen to be baseless, and have died out. The pastime is now as firmly established for women as it is for men.

With regard to the clothing worn while on the bicycle, it may be well to say a few words. The underwear should be as light as is consistent with warmth – all wool in winter, merino or gauze in summer. Any pressure about the body should be carefully avoided, and there should be no dragging from the waist. The shoes should be low-heeled and broad across the foot, boots should never be worn. The advantages of 'rational' dress have only to be experienced to be valued. It is possible to have an exceedingly neat, suitable and pretty costume in this mode, of tweed, cloth or serge – the knickerbockers slightly full, and the long buttoned leggings of the same material meeting them below the knee, the coat or tunic reaching half-way below the waist, or even lower, if desired. Where the now somewhat obsolete skirt is preferred, it should be made so as to entirely clear the feet when the rider is in the saddle. To have it long enough to incur a risk of the pedals catching in it as they revolve is to subject the rider to peril. An additional advantage in wearing 'rational' dress is that it obviates all need of a dress-guard, which increases the weight of a machine, and does not improve its appearance.

As to make, Frenchwomen have shown their preference for an entire avoidance of any skirt. They adopt a full blouse, or Eton jacket and shirt, very wide Turkish trousers, and often no leggings. Englishwomen have a style that in most cases adds to the moderately full knickerbockers, either a short knee-skirt, a long tunic, or an open coat with full skirt to it. Leggings almost invariably complete the costume, and should be of the same material as the knickerbockers. When riding, the French style looks smart and pretty, but off the machine the English fashion has decidedly the advantage. There is another point in favour of 'rational' dress, that it requires far less material than the long skirt, and is therefore considerably less expensive.

5

The Hygiene of Cycling

The rapidly increasing popularity of that form of exercise which is taken upon wheels, and the large number of persons of both sexes who have within the last few years become possessed of a cycle, has led to many inquiries as to the suitability of this kind of physical exertion for individuals of various ages and constitutions.

Much has been written by those who have practical experience of this pastime and by those who have not, and many contradictory opinions have been enunciated as to whether the bicycle and tricycle should be considered in the light of a boon or the reverse. In the following pages it is intended to discuss this question, and to formulate a few simple rules, also to give some hints as to riding, dress, diet etc. which may be useful to many who wish to ride but dread an injury to their constitution.

First of all, with regard to those who enjoy sound health, there can be no question that, whatever their sex or age, the exercise of cycling is in every way most beneficial. Though, of course, the muscles of the lower extremities are principally developed by the propulsion of the machine, they are not the only ones which are utilised. Those of the arms, back, shoulders and abdomen have secondary but important parts to play, while those which control the respiratory movements have a large amount of work thrown upon them, work which is enormously increased when the pace is fast or the road uphill. The pressure exercised by the large flat muscles of the abdomen also stimulates the many important organs which lie beneath. The heart of course participates in this increased action, and the improved circulation, both through the lungs and system generally, promotes reoxygenation of the blood, and that tissue change which is so essential to the maintenance of a sound state of health.

One of the most important questions with regard to cycling is whether young children should be allowed to ride, at what age they may begin, and how much they should do. It may be laid down as an invariable rule that no child with any organic weakness of heart, lungs, joints, or nervous system should be permitted to ride under any circumstances whatever. At an early age any such defect would be much accentuated by injudicious exertion, and permanent mischief very probably set up. But if a child be passed sound there is no doubt that moderate and properly regulated exercise on a bicycle or tricycle is one of the best forms of recreation for both sexes. It develops the body, and at the same time the self-reliance and resource entailed by the management of a machine strengthens and enlarges the mental and intellectual faculties.

Great care is nevertheless necessary, and a few simple precautions will insure good and avert evil. Some children are more forward than others, but as a rule an average boy or girl six years old may begin to learn to ride. To this rule, of course, there will be exceptions, but for the great majority it will be found appropriate. Great care should be exercised in choosing and fitting a machine for a young rider, as an unsuitable article might easily produce mischief, or even deformity. The machine must be light, the gearing low enough to permit of a short crank throw (four inches is generally ample for a child of six or seven), and the saddle and spring must be properly adapted to the weight and size of the rider. But most important of all is the length of reach. This should be quite short, the child should be able to touch the pedal easily with the heel when it is at its lowest point, for nothing is more injurious than a reach so long that the unfortunate boy appears as if riding on a rail, just touching the pedals with the tips of his toes. The position must also be carefully studied. Young growing tissues being easily distorted, a saddle too far back or handles too far forward would probably cause a curved spine and permanent 'camel's hump'. The peak of the saddle 1 inch behind the crank axle, and the handles so brought round and back that the child can sit perfectly upright on the machine, are two things that must be insisted on in buying either a bicycle or a tricycle for a young rider.

If these essentials be present, the question of tires is not so important, though, of course, some form of air tire is by far the best. The distance that may be safely ridden is a question which cannot be answered in miles and furlongs, as no absolute rule can be laid down, no two children of the same age being alike. The only thing that can be said is that anything more than moderate fatigue is injurious. A young growing child suffers much from over-exertion. Though at the finish of a ride he may seem fairly fresh, if he has done too much the results will be apparent soon after, and a sleepless night, with distaste for food, will show that the system is poisoned by its own waste. And it must be remembered, while treating of this subject, that excessive speed is more injurious than excessive distance – and excessive hill climbing than either. The great test by means of which a judgment may be formed as to the distance which is sufficient for each child is to observe:

1. How he sleeps the night after the ride.
2. How he takes his food
3. How he feels the day after. If he sleeps well, eats well, and is bright and lively the next day, the riding has not been pushed too far, and has done good, not harm, but if he is feverish and sleepless, refuses his food, and is languid, dull and thirsty the day after a ride, then it is certain that too much has been accomplished, and that such rides, if persisted in, will lead to mischief. In the case of children, as of adults, condition is, of course, attained by practice, and at the end of a few weeks the distance ridden may be increased with impunity.

To sum up in a few words, a sound child, six years old, properly fitted with a machine, and riding in proper form and position, may cycle within the limits of moderation, derive benefit, and suffer no harm from the exercise.

To pass to the other extreme of life, it may be asked what limit does age put to the enjoyment of this pastime? It is 'never too late to mend' so far as learning to ride is concerned, old men of eighty years and upwards have begun cycling, continued it for several years, and derived benefit from so doing. Of course a veteran of that age who, when well past the allotted span, starts a new athletic exercise is, in the great majority of cases, one who has used his body wisely and well, and consequently his muscular and circulatory systems are better prepared to stand the fresh strain thrown upon them than those of one who, having passed a sedentary and inactive life, takes up in his old age that physical culture which would have better become the days of his youth. While not actually forbidding sound and healthy individuals who have passed the rubicon of three score years to begin riding, great care should be inculcated. Old blood vessels are brittle, old muscles easily snap, and a moment's over-exertion may result in most serious injury. But guided by good sense and discretion, cycling exercise is better for an old man than too much armchair, and in many cases will improve the digestion, ward off rheumatism and prolong life. The late Major Knox Holmes, who began to ride in his seventy-fourth year, furnishes a case in point. He was a man who for the whole of his long life had been addicted to every kind of exercise, and when he was crippled with rheumatism had the energy to ride a tricycle, and continued riding until the day of his death. When eighty-three years old he stayed for some weeks at Hitchin, and enjoyed daily rides, some of great length, on the level stretches of road in that district, and at the end of the time it was found that he had actually developed fresh muscle, a thing almost unheard of in one of his years, while his general condition could only be described as perfect. Middle-aged riders, therefore, may take heart, and continue their favourite amusement in the certainty that 'age cannot wither nor custom stale its infinite variety' and that they are laying up for their old age a store of health and vitality which will carry them, active and full of vigour, well past the ordinary term of existence.

With regard to young girls and women learning to ride, much of what has been stated above applies. There is no reason whatever why they should not ride either a bicycle or tricycle, whichever may suit or please them best. For the great majority a bicycle is the more suitable, because it is both lighter and runs more easily, considerations not to be neglected in-the case of the physically weaker sex, and, more important still, is decidedly safer in case of accident. If a tricycle be upset a woman is terribly hampered, for being hemmed in by the handle-bar in front and the saddle-pillar and axle behind, she finds it exceedingly difficult to get clear of her machine, and has to fall with it. If, however, she be on a bicycle, and danger is apparent, it is comparatively easy to dismount, even when travelling at some speed, whether she be wearing a skirt and using the dropped frame, or, garbed in 'rational' dress, bestride a man's pattern of machine. Of course the one objection to a bicycle is the tendency of the air-tired wheel to slip sideways when ridden in greasy mud, and thus cause an awkward fall, but there are many fairly safe contrivances which reduce this risk to a minimum, and if one of these be employed the slight extra danger from this cause is more than compensated for by the increased convenience and handiness of a one-track machine, while, though the balance shortly becomes automatic, the extra care and attention required to manage a bicycle, which must be kept in motion, increases the rider's self-reliance, and is an excellent tonic for what are known as 'weak nerves'. For those, however, who find that increasing bulk and years render the act of mounting and dismounting irksome and difficult, the more stable three-wheeler must suffice, and they will discover that, if used with discretion, their reward in increased health and vigour both of body and mind is ample. For aesthetic reasons alone the upright position on the saddle, with the handle-bar sufficiently high and the ends properly brought round, should be insisted on in the case of every woman. The 'humped note of interrogation' attitude, with the saddle too far back, the reach too short, the handle-bar too far forward and dropped too low, is not only excessively unbecoming, but positively injurious, and if adopted by a young girl would soon permanently distort the spine, as well as cause other mischief more easily incurred than cured.

The distance that can be covered by a woman in a day, and the pace that can be maintained without injury or distress, depend in each individual on her skill, strength, and condition. One woman can ride 70 or 100 miles with less fatigue than is incurred by another in compassing 20, and one can battle with and conquer a hill, to attempt which dooms her sister to the sofa for a week. It should, however, be an absolute rule never to exceed the golden mean. Over-fatigue must be injurious, and for many reasons is more harmful to a woman than to a man.

No pastime, not even excepting horse exercise, is so calculated to raise the level and improve the tone of female health as the regular and judicious use of the modern cycle, confined within the bounds of due moderation. It banishes minor ills, strengthens the constitution, and many a girl now blooming with health owes her rescue from a life of invalidism to the beneficent magic of country air and regular exercise which the possession of an air-shod wheel has rendered possible.

It is very difficult to lay down any definite rules with regard to the cycling of the unsound. This is a matter which requires careful consideration in each particular case, and no invalid, or person with any organic physical lesion, should venture to ride without taking the best obtainable advice. The one thing that can be said in favour of the cycle as a means of obtaining that due amount of exercise which is sometimes needful, even in cases of grave illness, is that the weight of the body is rolled on wheels and the rider is relieved from carrying his own weight as well as having to propel it. This will be clear to anyone who will make the experiment of trying to carry a man of 12 stone weight on his back for a few hundred yards, and afterwards pushing the same person seated on a tricycle. In the first case the labour is irksome and soon becomes extremely fatiguing, especially if the pace is at all fast, in the second a mere push suffices, and a quick run can be maintained for a long distance with hardly more exertion to the pusher than if he were running alone. For this reason the exercise of cycling is particularly suitable to the weak and delicate, and many miles can be covered on smooth and level ground without the expenditure of more force than would be necessary to proceed a mile or so on foot. It is an actual experience that persons suffering from mild-valvular disease of the heart, who had been condemned to a life of inactivity, have derived benefit and improved their condition by gentle and regulated exercise on a machine. In such cases the muscle of the left side of the heart becomes increased in size, in order to enable that organ to overcome the difficulties which the defective valve places in the way of the due performance of its functions. Unless muscles, and especially enlarged muscles, are duly exercised, they are very prone to degeneration of their tissue. The heart-muscle is no exception to this rule, and if a person who on account of some lesion has to humour his circulatory system refrains altogether from that physiological use without which no organ can remain in an efficient and healthy condition, he will soon find that the efforts of nature to aid his damaged heart are in vain, that the enlarged muscle will decay, and his last state will be far worse than his first. But if he be well advised, and, while carefully refraining from all over-exertion, will give his heart just as much work to do as will keep it in the best and most healthy state possible, his general health will improve, while the local mischief will not be increased, but may even remain stationary for a longer time than it would under less favourable conditions. In such a case as this the use of a bicycle or tricycle is invaluable, it is far more beneficial than walking or riding, but it must be most dearly understood that any undue exertion will undo at once all the good that may be obtained by weeks of careful exercise. Level ground and a slow pace are essentials, the machine must be light and easy-running, and the gear low.

The ascent of hills must be scrupulously avoided, and every temptation to fast riding resisted. The distances which may be accomplished under such circumstances must be moderate, all fatigue considered harmful, and on no account should any risk of catching cold be run. The clothing should be loose and warm, and the position on the machine erect and easy. If a meal be taken while out it must be light and easily digested, and the saddle must not be resumed for some hour or more after its conclusion.

It does not by any means follow from what has been written above that it is advisable for every sufferer from heart mischief or disease of the circulatory system to mount a bicycle straightaway in the hope of thereby reaping benefit. There are some lesions of the heart in which such a proceeding would be sheer madness, and some diseases of the blood-vessels, such as aneurism, in which it might be instantaneously fatal. Each case must be judged on its own merits by a competent authority, and his decision unhesitatingly bowed to. As to mischief in the lungs and other organs essential to life, nothing need be added to what has already been laid down. In each class of disease there are some forms and some cases that will derive benefit from cycling exercise, with others in which it is entirely inadmissible, and it is quite outside the scope of such a work as this to formulate rules which may apply to any particular instance. For the blind nothing is more beneficial than a tandem steered by another rider having the use of his eyes, and the good work done at the Royal Normal College in providing recreation in this fashion for those who have lost their sight, and the excellent results in improved physical health obtained by the sufferers at that institution, speak for themselves in favour of urging the adoption of this means of exercise for all those who, though sightless, are otherwise sound and well.

A cycle worked by hand power alone is an unparalleled blessing to anyone who, either by accident or disease, has been deprived of the use of his legs, and many such instruments of different design are in constant use at the present time.

From what has just been stated it will be seen that the use of the bicycle in organic disease is somewhat restricted, but on turning to the much larger field of what are called 'functional' ailments it is apparent that there is great and increasing scope for its good offices, both in the way of prevention and of cure. Most of the disorders arising from the present advanced state of civilisation will yield to its influence, and it must be reckoned a deadly enemy to most of those symptoms which are popularly known as 'liver'. Gout and its first cousins, rheumatism, lumbago, and sciatica, fly before it, and it has recently been found a most useful adjunct to the course of treatment at various foreign watering places. In many cases of indigestion, and of the sleeplessness consequent thereon, it acts like a charm. After a country spin 'good digestion waits on appetite', the rider seeking his couch with a pleasant sense of fatigue finds the demon of sleeplessness exorcised, and awakes refreshed and fit for his day's avocations. No victim to 'nerves' can long resist the genial influence of a few hundred miles toured on a bicycle, and the fads and fancies dependent on that very uncomfortable condition will be dissipated into thin air after a very few days spent on the high road.

Young girls in their teens often suffer from 'bloodlessness' and a long train of consequent symptoms, and it will be found an invaluable aid to other measures taken to restore health if the sufferer be sent for a daily ride, and encouraged to use her machine, only taking care to avoid over-fatigue. Contrary to popular impressions, varicose veins and allied disorders are improved by cycling, and riders who suffer from rupture will not find their ailment increased, providing they use a proper truss, while it is difficult to see how this particular weakness can often originate from this cause.

There are also other functional derangements of the organs common to both sexes and special to each in which cycle exercise acts almost as a specific, and very many others in which a judicious and well-regulated use of it will much accelerate the process of cure, but this is a subject that can only be fully discussed in a purely medical work. It must suffice here to point out in a general way what a powerful weapon in the daily combat with invalidism is now placed in the hands of the medical profession, and to prophesy that it will be more and more extensively employed as the prejudice against this form of locomotion dies out, both in the minds of the faculty and their patients. And there are not wanting signs that this prejudice is now rapidly disappearing. The advent of the tricycle and the lowly 'safety' rendered it possible for men to cycle who could not afford to fall from the old high machine, and the later developments of the air tire and so-called 'rational' dress have drawn numbers of women to the wheel, especially abroad. Many physicians who, profiting by the athletic revival of the last thirty years, tasted the benefits of physical training in their youth, now in their maturity are anxious to confer the same boon on those who trust to their advice, and the old parrot cry that training and athleticism of every kind meant permanent injury is fast dying out, smothered by the practical and personal experience of many of the professors of the healing art.

It is not intended to refer at any length to the subject of dress in this chapter. This matter is very fully treated of in another part of the work, and it is only requisite here to insist on the necessity of all riders, both male and female, being loosely clothed. All tight bands and constrictions anywhere are harmful, and everyone who means to do anything more than merely play at riding must allow the chest ample room to expand. Discretion must also be exercised as to the texture of garments. Mischief has as often ensued from the use of too thick clothing in summer as of too thin in winter. With reference to the controversy, which is raging at the present time, as to the cycling dress of women, there can be but one opinion from a purely health point of view, and that is that the so-called 'rational' dress (i.e. knickerbockers and tunic) is far more suitable for athletic exercise of every kind than any arrangement of skirt or ordinary female garb that can be devised. So far as bicycle riding is concerned, it has the extra recommendation of greatly increased safety.

The question as to what constitutes the best form of diet for cyclists has provided a wide field on which the members of that large army of amiable faddists who are prepared at short notice to reorganise the human race have trotted out their several hobbies. The vegetarians pure and simple, the fruit-eaters, and those who support existence on vegetables tempered with milk, eggs, and cheese, together with the teetotalers and the moderate drinkers, have each in turn insisted that he who wishes to extract the greatest good from cycling must conform to that particular tenet regarding food and drink which is held by the professor who may happen at that time to be enlightening the listening world. Now, whatever might have been good and natural food for man in the days of our prehistoric ancestors, there can be no doubt that the nineteenth century representative of the race will thrive and flourish best on that form of food to which through countless ages that race has become accustomed, and to which his digestive system has gradually been modified. And looking at the teeth, the stomach, and other accessory portions of that system in present-day man, it is evident that he is best suited by, and will attain his greatest perfection on a mixed diet. The proportions of vegetable to flesh will vary, of course, in different climates and degrees of temperature, but it requires a human being with the stomach of a cow or the teeth of a lion to get the best results from a dietary exclusively consisting of meat or of vegetable. Let, then, the votary of the wheel eat and drink whatever he finds by experience suits him best, and live, while riding, in the same manner as any other rational being who takes his exercise on foot or horseback. The only alteration which bicycle riding should cause in his daily regiment is, that in a short time he may find that his improved digestive powers may permit him to indulge in articles of food which prudence would taboo when taking no active exercise.

What has just been written about food will apply word for word to drink. A man need not become a teetotaler, or, on the other hand, take to alcoholic drinks, because he cycles. If he be a water drinker, well and good, let him remain so, he will ride a bicycle none the worse. If he takes a moderate quantity of beer or wine at his meals, it will do him no harm. Excess in either direction is dangerous, and alcohol between meals is always bad. With regard to tea, coffee, cocoa, and such like beverages, experience must teach each individual what is best for himself. The great bulk of present-day riders are devoted to tea, some of the best racing men even drink it at dinner, and it does not appear to do them any harm. No absolute rule can be laid down as to what should be taken to drink between meals while actually riding on the road. Some simple non-alcoholic beverage is generally chosen, such as milk and soda water in equal proportions, the juice of a lemon squeezed into some 'fizzy' water, soda or lemonade, or mixed with cold tea without milk or sugar. Stimulants, such as brandy or whisky and soda and the like, are always bad, and should never be indulged in even if the rider be exhausted. He will be whipped up for the time, but after covering a few miles the inevitable reaction must set in, and leave him far worse than he was before. This rule also applies to long-distance races. Many a rider's chance in such a contest has been ruined by injudicious friends plying him with alcoholic stimulants. Great quantities of fluid should never be swallowed at one time. Such a practice spoils digestion, and does not effectually quench thirst. Drinks, again, should never be taken too hot or too cold, and it should always be kept in mind that 'quibus intumuit suffusa venter ab unda. Quo plus sunt potae, plus sitiuntur aquae'. It is a most important thing that a novice who is beginning to cycle, especially a youthful one, should be properly placed on his machine. The so-called 'scorcher attitude', with a bent body and humped back, is both wrong and injurious. It, however, still continues to exist among the unknowing, and not all the ridicule which has been showered upon it, nor even the dreadful term 'kyphosis bicyclistarum', with which it has been honoured, have sufficed to crush it out of existence.

In ordinary riding, even if the pace be fairly fast, the cyclist should sit upright and easily on his machine, the spine should always be kept quite straight, and the head erect. To insure this proper attitude the saddle must not be placed too far behind the crank axle, and the handle-bar should be sufficiently high and the handles brought so far round and back that they can be easily grasped without stooping. In riding against a heavy wind, or racing, it is of course necessary to bend forward so as to offer as little resistance as possible to the air. But there is a right and a wrong way of doing this. If the backbone be bent at an angle, and the elbows curved and held out from the sides, with the whole body stooping and the head hanging down, the position is most unscientific and injurious, cramping and contracting the chest, preventing the proper expansion of the lungs, and tending to produce a roundness of shoulders which might well drive a drill-sergeant to despair. But if the body be bent as a whole from the hips, with the spine perfectly straight, the shoulders rather back and the elbows kept in to the sides, then not only is the smallest possible surface presented to the opposing air, but the rider is in the position best adapted for filling the lungs. The body is instinctively held thus by sufferers from spasmodic asthma during the crisis of an attack. This position does not distort the body, and the vital capacity of the chest is increased rather than diminished.

A matter which frequently puzzles inquirers is that the regular practice of cycling sometimes has the effect of reducing and sometimes of increasing the weight of the body. The ex planation of these apparently opposite results is, however, simple. Professor Murchison many years ago showed that excessive leanness and excessive corpulence both arose from functional derangement of the liver, in the one case favouring and in the other preventing the absorption of the fatty elements of the food. May not beneficial exercise on wheels regulate the hepatic machine, and, promoting proper assimilation, insure the due proportional nutrition of all the bodily tissues? It must also be remembered that the 'too, too solid flesh' has a tendency to melt in perspiration, that the motive power for hard physical labour is mainly derived from the reserve stores of fat deposited in and about the frame, and also that an excessively spare man beginning work puts on more muscle, and consequently goes up in weight. The true reasons for the thinning of the stout and the building up of the lean must, therefore, be sought for in a combination of all the above-mentioned causes.

So long as young men remain what nature has made them, there will be those *quos curriculo pulverem Olympicum collegisse juvat*, and racing and other severe forms of athletic competition will be with us at the end as they have been from the beginning. Though the speed attained in races on bicycles is more than double that which can be reached by man's unaided efforts on his feet, yet the actual exertion is much less, and the exhaustion after a hardly contested mile race on wheels is not by any means so marked as after a foot-race of less than half that distance. This can be easily explained, as it is more labour to carry a weight than to roll it. The foot-racer carries his own weight, the bicyclist rolls it on wheels. This has already been referred to when treating of cycling for delicate persons. Other conditions in a race being equal, the greater the speed the greater is the effort on the part of the racer required to produce it, and consequently the fatigue and subsequent reaction is increased in proportion, and, providing the speed on either occasion be the same, a contest of one hundred miles entails twice the strain of one-half of that distance. In present-day racing the tendency is for both the speed and the distance competed over to increase, the drafts on the vital capacity of the contestants are therefore deeper, and the question whether such competitions are for the benefit of those who take part in them or not is forced into the foreground. As to racing, there are two rules which should be fixed and unchanged as the laws of the Medes and Persians. The first of these is that no person should ever be allowed to take part in a race unless he be properly trained, and the second is that no one should on any pretence whatever be allowed to train if he be in any way organically wrong. The pursuit of cycling has been advocated above as a means of improvement and even of cure in cases of delicate and unsound health, but racing on bicycles is a very different thing from the quiet easy riding there inculcated. The strain on heart, lungs, limbs, and nervous system involved in a hard and fast finish to a well-fought-out race is such that it can only be sustained with impunity by a perfect and sound machine brought by a judicious system of practice to the highest perfection of bodily health and condition, and any latent flaw which might have passed unnoticed for years under the conditions of ordinary life is bound, sooner or later, to become painfully or even fatally apparent under the stress of frequent and severe competition.

During the past two years some few women have competed in cycle races on the path, and others have ridden various distances against time on the road. This is not the place to discuss the ethical and aesthetic phases of this development. Whether the sight of a troup of scantily clad, perspiring, and exhausted females careering lap after lap round a race track, encouraged by the plaudits and subject to the jeers of that sort of crowd which would be attracted to such an exhibition, amid openly expressed criticisms, favourable or the reverse, on their personal proportions, and liable at any moment to a beauty-spoiling 'spill' – whether such a spectacle is likely to promote the good cause of healthy and recreative cycling among women or not, is a question which must be left to the good taste of those chiefly interested, and to the firmness and discretion of those governing bodies without whose permit such an entertainment cannot take place, except under the auspices of the professional showman. But it is right to speak out, and speak out plainly, as to the effects which such races would have on the health of the participants. Woman, as she exists in the present day, is not a racing animal.

What modifications in her form and economy nature might have effected had she been accustomed to violent and competitive outdoor exercise for the last few thousand years cannot now be told, but the result of her so-called 'subjection' is that in this nineteenth century she is utterly unfitted, whether she be 'new' or 'old' to undergo that continuous course of training without which, as has been stated above, no one, however strong or sound he or she may be, can engage in hard athletic competition except at the risk of incurring grave and perhaps permanent injury. The old adage that 'it is not the distance but the pace which kills' is more true in cycle racing than in other sports. It is quite possible for any healthy woman by regular and steady riding to attain such condition that she can accomplish 50, 60, or even a 100 miles in a day at a fair speed, and she may even keep up an average of 50 or 60 miles a day for some weeks and be all the better for it. But this is not the condition that is required to excel in the last lap of a path race. To reach the necessary fineness which will enable a competitor to hold her own in such a contest, a long, severe, and continuous course of work is necessary, and such an ordeal no ordinary woman can pass through without imperiling all her future health. Some of those who advocate the advent of women into' the athletic and cycling arena point out that she has participated with success in many other so-called manly sports, and instance riding, golf, hunting, shooting, rowing, and tennis. But all these pastimes differ essentially from racing, and even in some of these less harmful exercises mischief has resulted when they have been pushed to the point of competition, not so much from accidents while actually engaged in their pursuit as from ill effects only recognised in after years. Hunting alone is responsible for many a young life cut short, for years of pain among those of its female votaries who, carried away by enthusiasm and the spirit of emulation, have converted what should be a mere recreation into the main object of their lives. Let womankind take her part in every outdoor sport that is possible to her – she will improve her health and sweeten her days, but let her not attempt to fit herself for those trials of speed and endurance in which man alone, by reason of his strength and conformation, is able to indulge with impunity. By so doing she will reap all the good, and escape the after- math of repentance and suffering which always awaits these who infringe the laws of the great and good goddess Nature.

The CLASSIC GUIDE TO DATING

HENRY J. WEHMAN

978-1-4456-4419-6

THE CLASSIC GUIDE
TO
COCKTAILS

JERRY THOMAS

978-1-4456-4726-5

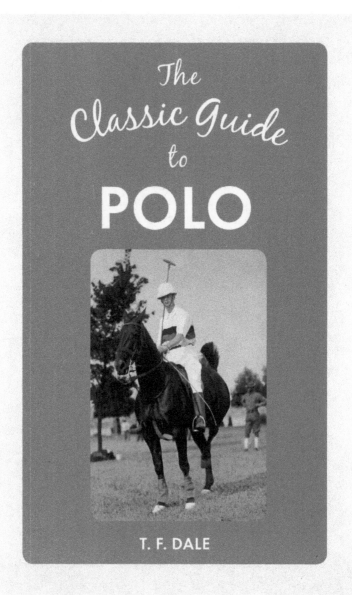

The
Classic Guide
to
POLO

T. F. DALE

978-1-4456-4866-8

The
Classic Guide
to
FLY FISHING

H. CHOLMONDELEY-PENNELL

978-1-4456-4723-4

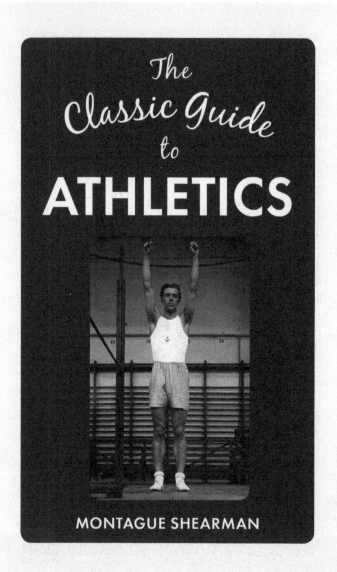

The

Classic Guide

to

ATHLETICS

MONTAGUE SHEARMAN

978-1-4456-4483-7